ISBN-13: 9798721964787

Cover design by: All 4 The Design
Library of Congress Control Number:
Printed in the United States of America

To My Knight on the White Horse: I could not have done this without you. Love you more.

To Mom, Dad, Dave, extended family and friends: Thank you for your continued support and for holding the reins as I take off on my life adventures. Love you all a bushel and a peck.

FOREWORD

I am the voice of the underdog. I speak to and for the people, departments, and groups that seemingly get passed over when it comes to learning the concepts of organization and continuous improvement. I know firsthand that all of these elements can work anywhere, and I will help to save you time (who doesn't want that?) and money (again... who doesn't want that?). No matter what your level of self-doubt is right now, I promise you: every single person can improve their daily lives through the processes explored in this book.

I am passionate about showing people how to apply continuous improvement concepts at home first, and then at work. I believe that if you can learn how to apply this stuff in your normal, day-to-day world, then you can implement the strategies at work as well. I have worked in manufacturing, in office settings, with large companies, and hand in hand with small businesses. In my head I have written this book a hundred times, and I have presented the material even more times than that to people in every situation, in every industry. I have loved every minute of it.

This is not a textbook, but I have written it as a reference guide for you to use early and often through your journey to make things better. It's written in everyday language with real life examples, like doing laundry, loading a dishwasher, and automating a report for work. I also often use stories about my family as examples (probably much to their dismay). So, please expect to hear my voice—and my humor—on the pages as you read.

I am grateful that my career veered off the original path, and I am blessed to land where I am today. I never could have imagined what was to come, or that you would be holding this book in your hands, about to learn how to improve absolutely anything.

To follow updates and examples from the book:

Web: www.howtoimproveabsolutelyanything.com

Facebook:https://www.facebook.com/
Howtoimproveabsolutelyanything

Instagram: howtoimproveabsolutelyanything

To follow me on any social media platforms:
Katie Labedz and Learning to Lean.

To work with the best writing coach in the world: Tricia Lott Williford, tricialottwilliford.com/

HOW TO IMPROVE ABSOLUTELY ANYTHING

Continuous Improvement in Your Home, Office, and Family

Katie Labedz

INTRODUCTION: KEYLESS ON A SNOWY MORNING

Sometimes the "Aha Moments" arrive quietly and conveniently. Sometimes they leave you locked inside a car you can't turn off.

My "Aha Moment" came on a snowy morning in Wisconsin as I rushed to get to work on time for the Thursday morning meeting. (Who schedules a meeting at 7:30 AM every Thursday, anyway?)

I scrolled through my mental checklist.

Laptop: Check.

Bag: Check.

Water: Check.

Coffee: Check.

Purse: Check.

My husband, Andrew, God bless him, got me all set and ready to go. He even told me I looked beautiful... so blessed to have a great hubby like that. He held my leather jacket open behind me, and as I slid my arms in the sleeves, he tenderly lifted my blonde hair, so it wouldn't get caught in the back of my coat. I tightened the belt on the jacket, hoping it would give me some resemblance of a waist, and I gave Andrew a hug and a kiss, and said, "I love you more."

The truck was already unlocked and warmed up. I checked again to be sure my laptop was in the back and my purse was up front, and I was ready to go. Andrew opened the garage door, and I backed out of the garage. As soon as I got to the circle, he shut the door and waved.

Man, I hate driving to work in the winter. Let's be honest, I hate winter.

I listened to country music on the radio, sipping my coffee that was no longer blast furnace hot. The heated steering wheel felt nice and warm, and so did my butt with the heated seats. You do whatever necessary to survive bone chilling winters in Wisconsin.

Careful, I reminded myself, as I came up to the corner and turned on Larsen. *This road is so slippery. Don't want to end up in the ditch like that big truck the other day.*

I checked my time as I waited at the light that always turns red when it sees me coming. Still doing okay, right on schedule, waiting for the light to change.

I felt a sinking feeling in my stomach as I got closer to the parking deck. Hmmm. *Just regular work nerves or something else. Did I see the keys for the truck in my purse?*

I was driving our new truck, the first one we've had that doesn't need an ignition key. Cool, but weird. I haven't yet gotten used to it.

I pulled into the parking deck and groaned—*ugh, someone took my spot!* I parked next to them with no time to walk from the upper deck today.

That creeping feeling was back. Something was unnerving me.

I shifted into park, and tried to shut off the truck.

Ding, ding, ding. That low mellow sound when the truck wants to tell me something. I noticed there was a light on the dash. *No key fob found!*

WHAT?! No key fob?? How did I drive all the way to work without it?

Why did it even let me shift into Drive? Ugh... bad process!!

NOW WHAT?!

I needed to call Andrew, and he wasn't going to be super happy about this.

I needed to text Jaime to say *I am going to be late for the meeting —because I'm sitting in the parking lot—and they will have to start without me.*

I speed dialed Andrew and explained my situation. "Andrew, I drove all the way to work without the car keys, and now I can't turn off the truck."

He asked the million-dollar question, "How did you do that?"

And then his solution, "Can't you drive back home?"

Grrrr... "Andrew, it's Thursday and you know I have to run the meeting at 7:30 AM. No, I cannot drive back home."

"Can't you leave it running while you're in your meeting?"

"In the parking deck? In the *PUBLIC* parking deck? No, I can't just leave it running here."

Ugh. Why didn't I check my purse when I got in the truck? I didn't follow my own process that I preach and teach about ALL THE TIME. Now it would take Andrew close to 30 minutes to get here, as long as the roads don't get worse.

"Yes, honey, please come help me. I am near my normal parking spot, right up at the top. Can't miss me...I'm in the white truck that's RUNNING!"

He was on his way to the rescue, and my thoughts rattled inside my head. *Do I even tell anyone at work about this? They will judge me, most definitely. Best bet is to call into the meeting from my phone. Good thing I looked at the projects yesterday. Fred will be pissed, John will judge. Don't anyone sit in my seat! I will be there in a few...I hope. How long will Andrew take to get here? I hope he doesn't dilly around, brushing his teeth, changing his clothes. Horses will be mad he is late. Hopefully he already fed the dog. Dang it... I screwed up everyone's morning over one simple thing. So stupid to have him waste an hour to come here and back.*

I tried to duck down in my truck so no one could see me sitting here, clearly not going in for the meeting. I sent them silent messages in my mind: *Don't anyone stop and try to talk to me. Please don't wait outside the truck! Move along, folks. Nothing to see here.*

Andrew called from that same stoplight I always get stuck at; it must turn red when it sees him, too. He was getting closer, coming over the bridge, and finally I could hear the diesel engine as he drove onto the parking deck. Andrew parked in the handicap spot and got out of the truck. I didn't have the emotional capacity for a tender moment of gratitude for my husband. I was watching the clock trying to listen in to the meeting through my phone, and I already had enough anxiety and felt dumb—*just hand me the keys, please.*

I took the remote and got in my truck, talking to the ignition. *Would you PLEASE shut off and get this nightmare over?* Turn it off, on and off again. All set. This time I clip my keys to my purse—*the task I should have done earlier this morning.*

I grabbed my purse and my bag, ready to run into the meeting. Of course, after sitting there for so long and finishing my coffee... I had to pee!

I hurried through the cold, barged into the building and through the employee entrance. I ran to the bathroom, careful not to slip on the wet floor, dumped my stuff on the wood bench in the locker room, and rushed into a stall. At the last second, just before my sense of relief, I thought, *Katie! Make sure you are on mute! I don't need the entire world to hear me peeing.*

(How do you balance your phone while peeing, anyway? We need a process for that.)

I washed up, grabbed my things, and dashed to the elevator. *Should I rush into the meeting I'm already late for? Should I go to my office first and dump my stuff and my jacket? People will stare regardless, but even more so when I look like a wreck with my baggage in tow. Office it is!*

I dropped it all on my desk, took off my coat, grabbed the laptop, and raced to the finish line.

I glanced at my watch once more. It had been a REALLY long day already... and it was only 8 AM.

Maybe you are thinking, "Been there, done that."

Okay, perhaps you haven't been unable to turn off your car, but have you made a silly mistake that could have been avoided with a routine process? Does something similar happen to you *all the time*? Do you have a recurring task at home or at work that bugs you to complete it? When was the last time you took inventory and organized your life?

I will show you some amazingly easy concepts that can help you improve these situations and many more. You can learn how to use these processes at home first (because let's face it, lately we are spending A LOT of time there) and then how to implement them at work.

Are you thinking right now, "I am NOT an organized person, and I can't do this. Can I return this book to Amazon?"

Hear me well: Yes, you are an organized person, and I can prove it.

Do you have a utensil drawer organizer? You know, the one with the designated spots for the forks, the knives, and the spoons? I'm guessing you do (unless you use chopsticks, because even store bought plasticware is divided up in the box).

Here's a guarantee: If you can use that utensil drawer organizer every day of your life, through childhood and all the way into adulthood, then you have proof that you can learn a process, stay organized, and improve anything in your life!

Before we get too far ahead of ourselves, let's talk about continuous improvement, the basis and foundation for this book.

What is continuous improvement? Continuous improvement is a circle with no end, the constant cycle of making things better. Continuous improvement makes the world go round, and we can watch its evolution in our progress from rotary dial phones to cordless phones, bag cell phones, and now our super smartphones. Continuous improvement means always striving to make things better for ourselves, our families, our employees, our customers. And when we make this one thing better, we look for something else to improve. There is always a process that can be tweaked, tightened, and improved for greater success and efficiency.

Continuous Improvement is a circle with no end, the constant cycle of making things better.

The ideas in this book are based on the concepts of continuous improvement and Lean ideas, and they can help to eliminate a lot of your "oh-shit" moments. I'm here to tell you that I'm doing them, too. I really do practice what I preach... even though life does sometimes get in the way, and I find a process of my own that needs a complete overhaul. (Hello...car keys.)

Everyone—yes, everyone—in every role, every house, every company, and every industry in the world can benefit by applying these concepts. This book is going to save you time AND money. No magic potion required. I promise.

Ready to learn more and improve your life? Go look at that utensil drawer organizer to find your inspiration, and let's go!

CHAPTER ONE: IT'S NOT ALL ABOUT MANUFACTURING

Continuous Improvement is for All of Us

I originally wanted to title this book *Continuous Improvement for the 'Rest of Us'*.

And by "the rest of us," I am talking about those of us who are at home, or at work in a non-manufacturing capacity, like HR, Finance, IT, Supply Chain, Ops, and administrative functions. The ideas we will walk through are traditionally created for a manufacturing environment, but, guess what, they work for the rest of us, too. The "carpet walkers," parents, teachers, mechanics, lawyers, doctors, etc.

Truly, the rest of us.

Most companies begin their improvement journey in manufacturing because they think they can achieve "quick wins" or attack "low hanging fruit" or get "more bang for their buck." In reality, they start there because it is easier to see improvements on a manufacturing line. You can literally see the changes with your actual eyeballs when you are walking by. *Oh, look! There was a machine here yesterday and not one today! The line was rearranged and now we have a bunch of extra floor space. How cool!*

Some improvements are not as obvious.

When you walk down the aisle of the IT department, you can't see that the report that once required 19 hours to complete is now automatically done (with no errors) in under two minutes. (True story of a real example).

You can look at the final sales numbers and financials for the month, but you can't see that the process now requires only half of the software than before.

And, let's face it, dinner guests don't come into your house to "ooh and aah" at your newly organized pantry or linen closet.

It's tempting to focus on only the changes we can see, but when you know the improvements are there even if they're invisible, it's satisfying. And it makes your life easier.

We apply these concepts at home all the time. (But, maybe, don't tell my husband that. He is the brunt of many of my stories and often my "guinea pig.") We use these concepts of continuous improvement for laundry, managing pets (dogs, cats, horses), running two businesses, and even successfully moving across the country—twice.

I'll never forget our move from Florida to Wisconsin, a relocation that is literally halfway across the country, at least when you look from the bottom of the map to the top. That season was a flurry of activity: working with relocation specialists, selling a house, buying a house, a once-in-a-lifetime trip to Poland for hubby and me, and, oh yeah, we have three horses, a dog, and two cats to move, plus a workshop, a pontoon boat, and a tractor. Not my definition of a relaxing tea party.

We put out an "all call" to our friends and parental units...we need some help!

We put our team together. Mom and Dad would come to Florida first and take all the documents and fragile items back with them to Michigan, and then they would meet me in Wisconsin. Our friend, Howie, agreed to come down and help Andrew move the horses, cats, trailer, pontoon boat, and the tractor.

I made the first trip because I had to get settled in Wisconsin so I could start my new job which was the whole reason for the transition. Then, as I was settling into my new job and my new routines, everything started arriving in stages. Andrew made two trips back and forth between Florida and Wisconsin. Andrew arrived with his first trip, the horse trailer full of hay, and the dog. The horses came next, and the parental unit planned to get here in time to help with them. Andrew's final trip up was with Howie. Andrew was towing the tractor and Howie was towing our pontoon boat. Finally, the movers arrived.

In other words: Complete and Utter Chaos.

As I got home from work each day, there were boxes and people *everywhere*. My parents and Andrew were so proud of what they were able to accomplish, and they were eager to show me their progress. Yes, I was grateful for the help, but *OMG!*

Mom decided to start organizing the kitchen and put things away on her own, fueled by the concept that if the kitchen is put away, then the whole house can begin to function normally. Maybe...but let's be honest. When I've just moved hundreds of miles with a herd of animals to a new state with a vastly differing climate, and started a new job, the last thing I wanted to do was spend time in the kitchen cooking!

It was finally time—maybe long past time—for the parental units to head home, back to Michigan. I was eager to be alone with Andrew again, just the two of us in our new home, new place, new life.

That means it was time for me to start cooking again, but since someone else had organized my kitchen, I didn't know where to find anything. My kitchen hardly felt like it was *mine*.

I would come home every day, start the dinner plan, and have to call my mom to ask where shit is. Andrew had no clue, he wasn't in the room when she was unpacking my stuff, so I'd have to call Mom again and again and ask, "Mom, where are the glasses? How about the plates? Where is my favorite spatula?" (Face it: we all have one.)

I was SO frustrated. The kitchen (and the horse barn) are my kingdoms, and I was lost without my systems. I had NO IDEA where to find anything, and I could not decode any logic to the madness.

Take a breath, Katie. Everyone was only trying to help. But really...

why are the cups here and not over there? Why are the pots like that?!

Mmmm, well, there is this: I am 5'6", my mom is 5'2" (and shrinking), and hubby is 6'. While organizing my kitchen, everything found its home either at mom's eye level or hubby's. Which means that everything was either several inches shorter or taller than me. The only thing between those two heights was the utensil drawer organizer. Each day I wasted so much time searching cupboards and drawers for *this* utensil or *that* pan, all with no time to really "fix" the problem since I had so little time at all, given the new job, a whole house still in shambles, and—oh, yeah—still trying to sell the house in Florida.

My frustration turned into anger. Yes, *anger* over where my loaf pan was hiding. Crazy, sure, but please tell me you get it. One weekend in the dead of our first Wisconsin winter, in a cold that my bones hadn't felt in over 10 years living in Florida, I snapped. I couldn't do it anymore! I could not spin in circles for one more day, looking down at chest level or far above my head. I had had enough. I removed every single item out of every single drawer, cupboard, and shelf, and I started over again.

I held each item in my hands, and I made decisions. What do I use the most? Where is the most logical place (in my mind—based on *my height*) to put it? I found a few pans I hadn't used in years, and I encountered a few items I didn't recognize at all. If I hadn't used it or didn't know how to use it, I tossed it or donated it.[1]

With each decision I began to breathe easier.

Has this ever happened to you? Has someone tried to "help" you at home or at work? How about that caring partner or teammate who "tries to make your life easier" by rearranging your closet or even your desk?! They may have tried to show you "the right way" to load the dishwasher or "the correct way" to fold towels, and you might be ready to lose your ever-loving mind over it. You know you already have the ability to make things more efficient (hello... utensil drawer organizer), but someone wants to butt in and offer their two cents.

Maybe you are thinking to yourself right now, "Katie, I am SUPER organized. I've got this, and I really don't need your help (hello...refund!). My processes are perfection. I have watched all of the YouTuber's and Instagram Queens on this. I've got it."

And maybe you do. But let me ask you this question.

Did you know the average process contains 95% waste?!

What?! Yes, you read that correctly. Only five percent of the steps that you take to complete a process add actual value to your end product. Shocking, I know.

Waste (and now you know you have a lot of it, too) is anything that utilizes resources but adds NO value. That means it doesn't make your end product any better, whether that end product is a printed sales report or a packed school lunch. Just like you take the waste out to the curb every Monday at 7 AM, you want to remove waste from your processes. We will look at the different types of waste, and I will show you how to kick it to the curb and improve your processes to make your home, work, and life more efficient.

Consider this:

What would you do if you had an extra 2 ½ hours a month? What could your business do with an extra $1M a year? Yes, that's what I'm talking about. That's what efficiency and continuous improvement can give you: time and money. Who doesn't want that?

Continuous improvement is an overarching look at making things better. Under the umbrella of continuous improvement, there are two main concepts: Lean, and Six Sigma.[1] Lean focuses on the elimination of waste from a process, thereby making what is needed, when it's needed, with the least amount of waste. For example, making just enough spaghetti to feed two people, not six! Or printing out one permission slip, not four, "just in case you lose a few."

Six Sigma,[2] in its simplest definition, is a mathematical approach to problem solving. That's my softer, kinder, gentler description of Six Sigma. (If I told you that it is a statistical approach to problem solving following a prescribed methodology, you might just toss the book across the room right now, and I want us to stay friends.)

Don't worry. We are going to focus on continuous improvement and Lean concepts for the majority of the book. No math required!

With the concepts of continuous improvement and Lean, you can improve absolutely anything. In the following chapters we will talk about translating traditional manufacturing concepts into ideas that we can all understand and apply. We will look at cellular flow (how a manufacturing line is arranged on a manufacturing floor), and I'll show you how to apply this to your desk at work—or your kid's desk at home. We will also talk about the concept of 5S, an organizational method to help determine where you should place things on your desk, in your workshop, or even in your kitchen.

Start thinking about opportunities or areas where you'd like to improve. Maybe it is the kitchen setup, the linen closet, or that dang report your boss wants every week. Let me help you weed through the chaos and show you where to begin.

CHAPTER TWO: WHERE TO BEGIN?

Start the Journey

Start by thinking about the process or situation that BUGS[3]21 you the most. I mean, one that really gets under your skin. Maybe it's the cycle of washing, drying, and putting away laundry. Maybe it's preparing dinner and cleaning up afterward. Maybe it's that dang report you dread working on for your boss every Friday (due by 10 AM). That "thing," that process or task that bugs you the most, that is where you begin your improvement journey.

That's where I started, too; in the horse barn.

We have three horses. Well, technically we have 2 ½ horses: a draft horse (big guy named Secret), a blind, off-the-track thoroughbred (Delta), and a mini donkey named Wilbur. We rescued him from a pig farm, hence the name from *Charlotte's Web*.

Living in the Great White North they need horse blankets (or jackets) during the winter. We only use their blankets when it gets dang-cold (a technical term that applies to approximately six months out of the year) or when there is freezing rain. (By the way, all of the horse blankets in the world seem to be either green or blue, both of which show all the dirt, mud, and wear. Why, horse blanket makers? Why??)

Each of the horses has at least two blankets: a lighter one (like a rain jacket, also called a sheet), and a heavy one (like a parka, complete with Thinsulate material). The blankets are stored high on a shelf off to the right side of the aisle in the barn. The shelf is waaaaaay up there, like six feet off the ground, with bi-fold doors to close it up, just so we don't have to see a giant pile of these blankets all the time.

When it's blanket time here in Wisconsin, I have to climb up a ladder, pull all the blankets down off the two shelves, figure out whose is whose, and separate the lighter blankets from the heavier. In the past we had tried to make organized "piles" of blankets, with Delta's on the left, Secret's on the right, and Wilbur's on the top. That didn't seem to work very well because I still had to pull down each pile for every horse. (Again, they are all blue or green, and in the dark aisle, they all look the same. I'm looking at *you*, horse blanket makers.)

It's frustrating to say the least. In the cold my fingers don't want to work, and—let's face it—when one is blindly pulling giant horse jackets off a high shelf in a barn, one can only guess what will fall on top of her in the process.

I am happy to give you this tip: Amazon came to the rescue! Amazon has clear, handy plastic bags with handles that zip up to close sort of like the bags that a new comforter would come in. I'll take six, please.

Now I could create a process. First, I pulled down all the blankets separating them by type and by horse. I found a few that don't fit any of our horses, random no-name horse blankets that were probably hubby's great "find" at a garage sale. I set them aside in a pile to donate.

Next, I grabbed some colored labels, tape, and some markers, and away I went! On the top and side of each bag I labeled the name of the horse and the type of blanket tucked inside. Of course, the labels are color-coded: pink for Delta, orange for Secret, and white for Wilbur. I folded up the blankets, tossed in a few dryer sheets for freshness, zipped up the bags, and placed them on the shelf once again. Now anyone can clearly see what we have stocked and stored for each horse, and we are able to quickly find what we need.

I recently tested this a few weeks ago when a cold front came through Wisconsin, and I'm glad to tell you the process worked perfectly. I smiled inside and out with a huge sense of accomplishment. Of course, the horses looked at me funny and couldn't have cared less. They just wanted to be warm and dry, and they don't really appreciate my organizational skills. But my personal sense of satisfaction soared to the moon.

So, what bugs you the most? (We are not talking about the *people* that bug you the most—that's someone else's specialty, not mine!)

Maybe you're not irritated by messy horse blankets, but what about your vehicle with papers, wrappers, receipts, and miscellaneous food items? How about the endless task of trying to remember the 10,000+ passwords for every system, every website, and every app you have ever used? Wouldn't you love to have a more organized backpack, purse, or diaper bag? How about actually finding what you are looking for in there, instead of rummaging around the "black hole" of a bag, only to find a smushed granola bar and bent paperclips way down at the bottom, when all you really needed is a pen?

I'd like to teach you an extremely easy concept to get organized. Yes, you can do this, you savvy owner of a utensil drawer organizer.

Start small. Begin with the annoying task that bugs you the most.

The concept is called 5S. Quite cleverly there are five steps in this process, and each step starts with the letter *S*. (Imagine that.) The steps are: Sort, Set in order, Shine, Standardize, and Sustain.

The concept of 5S has been around since before Henry Ford and originated in Japan.[4] You may have heard the common adage of this concept: "A place for everything, and everything in its place." The idea behind this concept is to identify a place for everything, and then return everything to its designated space: like having a designated "parking spot" in your vehicle for your sunglasses, a bin on your kitchen counter to store receipts, or that giant water container in the corner of your closet where you can toss your loose change. Life is much more organized when everything has its own place where it belongs.

Try this with me.

Sort. In this step we (physically or virtually) sort the collection into two piles: Keep or Toss.

You have probably seen this process in play. If you've done Whole 30, then you know the first step is to go through all of your food and remove what you aren't going to need for the next 30 days. And do you remember that HGTV show that made the participants do this very same thing with a cluttered space that had gotten out of control? Now it's your turn.

It's time to dump that bag, take everything off your desk, empty out the closet in your spare bedroom, or open up the home screen on your laptop, and make some decisions. Pull that car-truck-minivan-mini-something into the driveway, garage or barn, and pull everything out of it. Yes, *everything*. Including the floor mats that haven't seen the light of day in...*years*.

Ask yourself, and answer honestly: Do you *really* need everything there? Why do you have a power charger for the cell phone that broke and was replaced two years ago? How about the 74 virtual folders on your desktop? I know you *think* you can find everything you are looking for on there, but let's be real, shall we?

Choose a task you can realistically accomplish in one day.

By the way, it's okay if this takes you a while to accomplish. And by "a while," I mean it's okay if it takes all of one day— NOT all week, all month, all year, or multiple years. As you decide where to begin, choose a task you can realistically accomplish in a day, or you will lose your motivation and all your momentum.

Now that we have a Keep and a Toss pile, decide RIGHT NOW what to do with that Toss pile. Move it out to the garage, put it in a box or a bag, whatever you decide, get that stuff out of sight and out of mind, so you won't feel tempted to bring it all back in. There are hundreds of worthy causes that can turn your toss pile into treasure or money for those in need.

Congratulations. Now you have only your Keep pile, and really, that should be a significant smaller pile of "stuff" than when you started.

Set in Order. Now that you have cleared off that desk, closet, purse, car, or desktop take a logical and intentional look at where to place your remaining items.

This may cause you to ask yourself questions you may have never considered. Where is the most efficient spot for your computer? Can you realistically and comfortably reach your desk phone (yes, some offices still have those) from where you are seated? Which side of the screen on your laptop desktop do you "favor"? (I like the left.) What do you most often reach into your purse to find? (Mine is a toss-up between my credit card and lipstick.) What's the most common item that you reach for in your backpack? (For me, it's my laptop, my mouse, and my power cord.) In your car where can you place your umbrella or ice scraper so you can easily reach it in inclement weather?

Don't put them in place yet – just decide in your mind where you want them to go. Envision the most optimal place for all your remaining items. Don't worry if you don't get it right on the first try. Remember, this is *continuous* improvement, a circle with no end. There will always be a little bit of waste in your process, and you can work to remove that later on.

Shine. Yay! Now it's time to clean up the area before you put all your stuff back. You don't want to put your things back on a dusty desk or into a backpack still full of crumpled paper and crumbs of granola bars from days gone by. (Yep, that's mine.) Take a moment to shine.

I remember walking into a manufacturing plant that obviously DID NOT practice 5S at all—certainly not recently, maybe not ever. Nothing was organized. There were parts stacked everywhere with no labels, no order, and no cleanliness. The place was DIRTY. I approached a kind lady working on the line, and I asked if they take time to practice 5S, not because I am a witch, but because I wanted to define their perception of clean and organized. The lady responded, "Yes, we do! We clean our work stations every day at 3 PM!" And she held a Windex bottle up to my face as proof.

Ah...okay. That explained a lot. That's not exactly 5S. They had a solid 1S going on there. You need to implement the other four to make this process work.

Take a few minutes to dust, dump, vacuum, wipe down, or even change the background picture on your desktop from the standard Windows blue to something more pleasing. (I have a picture of my handsome hubby on my desktop because he makes me smile.) You do you.

Standardize. You want to create a standard placement of the items in your now super clean location. Remember, you already thought about this during your Set in Order step, and now it's time to put things in place.

Slide the laptop into the padded slot of your backpack or into the pocket most convenient for you. Move the phone from the far left corner of your desk to the right side instead, in case you just remembered that you are right-handed! Place the desktop icons in a logical order. I actually have less than 10 icons on my desktop, and I could probably minimize that even further, since I use my taskbar 99% of the time anyway. (Oh, look—another opportunity for improvement for me!)

You can get as specific as you choose with your standardization. I once knew an engineer at Chrysler who used colored tape to indicate *exactly* where the phone should be on his desk. Like I said, you do you.

Reuse before you buy and buy cheap before expensive or fancy.

Before you go shopping for organizational supplies, I strongly encourage you to first look for bins and baskets in your own home. See what you can reuse before you buy new. Even some of those containers in the kitchen—the ones whose lids have gone to live with some of your missing socks—can be repurposed. If all else fails, go to a dollar store or even a thrift store. This experience does not have to be expensive by any means. Trust me, I get giddy walking into the store dedicated to organization, but I can't afford all those fancy bins for my home and work life. In my desk right now I have five bins that I picked up from the local dollar store, and that cost me—you guessed it—five dollars. Reuse before you buy, and buy cheap before expensive or fancy.

When you think you have completed the Set in Order step, take a moment to review what you have accomplished. Be sure it makes sense to you, and consider whether you can live with it for now (or until you improve it later on). If you see something that you want to move or change, do that now. Don't wait until later. Do it while you are in the moment, while you can see what you want to improve.

If you are brave you can ask your partner, friend, or co-worker for their opinion, as they may have some ideas you haven't considered. Personally, I prefer to walk away for a few minutes, give myself a break, and then come back to look at it with fresh eyes. I honestly don't want anyone else's opinion of my hard work, and I will only get irritated if they try to improve on my "masterpiece." Best for me to avoid that whole conversation.

Sustain. I am not going to lie to you: this is the hardest step. Sustain means "keeping this up." It means continuing to keep your desktop clean, and not adding more icons because you are in a hurry to save that file. It means putting your pens away in that one dollar bin every day. It means putting your credit card away in your wallet (or newly designated location) *every time* you are finished using it.

Back in the 1960s Dr. Maxwell Maltz[5] shared his observation that it took, on an average, a minimum of three weeks for people to adopt a new habit, and the world ran with the optimism of how much could change in 21 days. Recent studies have bumped that number up to 66 days, and one of the most significant studies showed that it can take anywhere between 18 and 254 days.[6] The whole point: it doesn't happen overnight. Change like this can be hard and uncomfortable since it is MUCH easier to revert back to the way we have "always done it."

Continuous Improvement is an ongoing commitment to make something better for you, your family, and your customers. Your family would appreciate a less stressed parent, and your customers will feel more confident if you are organized while you're pulling up data, presenting from your computer, or even driving them to lunch in your vehicle. You won't regret the time you spent to strengthen this part of your life.

I challenge you to commit to the new habit for two weeks. Just 14 days—*but,* it has to be 14 days total. Fourteen times to get it right. For example, I don't use my credit card every day (which makes for a happy husband), so 14 days of relearning to correctly put away my credit card took longer than two consecutive weeks.

Remember, you've got this, you successful owner and user of the utensil drawer organizer. If you can properly put your forks away, then you can Sort, Set in Order, Shine, Standardize, and Sustain.

How do you define "value" in your world? What do you value? It's different for everyone.

I value time, but my hubby values efficiency. My parents value simple, uncomplicated instructions. I have one friend that values money and another who deeply values a good night's sleep (she's the parent of twin babies). There is no right or wrong answer to this. For goodness sake, some people still value Chia Pets, or they wouldn't keep making them.

Our values can change in various seasons of life, and they shift also with the evolution of new inventions. For example, people once told time by using a sundial, then a pocket watch, then a windup wristwatch. They progressed to a digital wristwatch, and now so many of us pay top dollar for a "fitness app/heart rate monitor/fall detector/step counter/buy your coffee/watch." The theme throughout is a consistent value: keeping track of time. How it manifests in our lives, well, that grows and changes.

I establish my processes because I value TIME in my life. The faster and more efficient I can be, the more time I allow myself to work on other things that I find valuable, like furthering my knowledge, exploring my creativity, riding our horses, and traveling with my hubby on our motorcycles.

What you value is important to you, but you should also be able to identify the values of your boss, your customers, and your partner. In a traditional sense, value is something that a "customer" is willing to pay for. It transforms a product or improves a service, and it is done right the first time (more on this in Chapter 16). So, yes, I value my new battery operated heated gloves that arrived at my house the day after I ordered them. The batteries were fully charged and ready to go when I opened the box. My hubby would never value anything like that, and that's okay, too. What you value will motivate what you seek to improve.

Take a moment to figure out what "bugs" you the most, and usually you'll find that it points to something you value. The concept of *5S* equips you to improve that process so it's even *more* valuable to you.

CHAPTER THREE: LET THE CIRCLE BEGIN

Plan, Do, Check, Act

I am willing to consider the possibility that your first improvement process may not have "stuck." In fact, it may have actually "stunk."

Been there, done that, even after 14 days of trying to make it work.

Maybe you had an impromptu carpool with an associate, and you had to throw shit in the backseat before you could allow them to ride with you as a passenger. Maybe you're ready to make a purchase for your home or office, but you cannot for the life of you find your credit card. You meant to put it back, but it's missing...again.

It's okay. You've got this.

Let me teach you another process, a circular practice called Plan-Do-Check-Act (PDCA), that will help make those changes stick—or help you to start over when it's time to shake things up again. Remember, 95% of our processes are waste, so we have endless opportunities to improve!

Plan. The first step calls you to *really* understand the problem you are trying to solve. Most of the time, when people come to me for help with a process, 80% of the conversation is their emotional response, and only 20% is factual data. While I have compassion for their frustration, I need to help them identify the actual problem before we can resolve this situation.

What problem are you trying to solve? Be specific. Are you trying to lose weight? Are you trying to reduce the amount of time it takes you to review your emails in the morning? How about finding a faster way to cook dinner at night? Identify the problem you are trying to solve, and then bring on the data!

You need your starting data. Anytime we track something, we need to know where we started. A few examples of data in everyday life:

- When the pitcher comes to the mound at a baseball game, the announcer tells us his stats—his current wins, strikeouts, and shutouts. These numbers will change by the end of the game, so it's important to know his data and stats when he steps up to the mound.
- The dashboard of your vehicle has a mileage display to indicate the average miles per gallon when you turn the ignition for the first time each day. The gauge shows year-to-date or current gas mileage.
- When you log into your HR system at work, it will show you how many vacation days you have available as of that day.

All of these numbers are called baseline data. This is where we begin. Without it we have no idea whether our improvements and adjustments have made things better or worse. (Yes, even your good intentions can sometimes make things worse.)

Spend 50% of your time in the Planning stage.

Don't rush this step.

Quite literally one of the greatest measures of your success begins with your starting data. In fact, when you begin a PDCA cycle, you should spend 50% of your time in the planning stage. This is NOT a ready-fire-aim sort of activity. The planning stage may feel like an excessive amount of time, but this step is going to pay off tenfold in the future.

My parents are senior citizens, and they don't always adapt

well to change. Honestly, what they value most are processes that remain the same. When anything changes in their world, they panic and call me.

Earlier this year, they received the renewal notice for their vehicle registrations, and lo and behold, the process had changed. You can no longer go to the Secretary of State for an in-person transaction. Instead, it all happens in an updated, automated process at a kiosk in the grocery store. My parents swore they had never seen this big bright yellow kiosk. They worried about how long the process will take, the payment method, how many people could be in line in front of them, whether the credit card reader will work, will it dispense the registration AND the plate sticker, etc. My dad was ready to call the Governor's office to file a complaint first thing Monday morning.

I could have told them, and you probably agree, that the kiosk process is actually much more efficient. When the State of Michigan required all vehicle registration and license plate renewals to be processed in person at the local Secretary of State, my parents spent an average of 45 minutes to complete the renewal process for three vehicles. The new kiosk process now takes them less than five minutes to complete for three vehicles, and it's less than five minutes from home. But they were not interested in these facts yet.

There was a whole lot of talking before we could identify the actual problem they were trying to solve: how to overcome the fear of change and establish a clear understanding of a new process. That's not a government problem; that's a life skill.

It takes time to weed through the emotions of problem solving, but if you rush through this step, you'll find yourself on a path to solving the wrong problem.

Do. This is when you actually get to work on solving that problem! Lots of people are eager to work on the fix before they truly understand the problem and current situation, and I like to call that Problem Solving Paintball. If you keep aiming and shooting big blobs of solutions at a random target, you'll end up with a sticky mess and no problem solved. Once you have a clear target in sight, that is the time to Do.

Here is the most important thing to keep in mind for this step: You are looking for a "minimal viable product."[7] What does that mean? You make your most educated guess based on the information you have, but don't get paralyzed by trying to get it 100% right the first time.

I know that landed like a crushing blow to all of the perfectionists in the world. (I deeply understand. I, too, am a recovering perfectionist). Continuous improvement is ongoing, so you get more chances to make it *right*! Make one small change, and trust the process. This is not a one-time shot.

Check. This step allows you to take a step back and see if this change really solved the problem, if there is at least a small improvement, or if you may have made the problem *worse*. Compare your new information with the baseline data from your Plan step, and you can verify whether your process has improved.

- Did the pitcher increase the number of strikeouts in this game? If we know how many she/he had to start with, we will know if the change in their pitch improved today's game.
- When you're planning your most efficient route to work, you can tell if your mileage has improved because you can compare it to the mileage when you started keeping track.
- When you plan your vacation time for the year, you know if you have enough time remaining because you know how many days you started with.

Act. This step allows you to determine what to do next. Should you keep the new process, or go back to the Plan step and start again? The Act step allows you to make a decision.

Keep improving, learning and doing. The only poor outcome is to be paralyzed by fear and make not changes at all.

If the results are not as you expected, that's okay. You have made progress even as you learned what doesn't work. That's why PDCA is a circle with no end. You keep improving, learning, and doing, and it never has to be perfect the first time around. The only poor outcome is to be paralyzed by fear and make no changes at all.

Now, let's take a look at how you can use PDCA in "real life."

Problem: The Number on the Bathroom Scale

Let's say you are trying to lose weight. (Or maybe you're trying to gain some weight—lucky you!) It's the new year and the new you!

Plan: Focus on the problem to solve, and gather starting data. Ask good questions:

Why do you want to lose weight? Be specific. Perhaps you want to improve your health and lower your cholesterol or A1C numbers, or maybe you'd like to fit into that favorite pair of jeans you have had on the shelf since the beginning of 2000.

What is your starting weight today? Whether you're aiming to lose or gain, you need to know your current weight (yeah, I hate that part too) and your goal weight (or at least your first goal). Your current weight is 180 (our baseline data-let's be real here people on what most of us weigh). Your goal weight is 170 (very realistic goal weight).

Do: Make one change. Maybe you decide to start by eliminating your late night snack habit, and stop drinking pop. (I am from Michigan, so it's not soda. It's pop). Take action toward your goal.

Check: For a weight loss journey, don't check your progress until two weeks after you've made your changes. *Two weeks,* people, *not two days*. It takes time to see changes in a weight loss routine. After two weeks take a look at your results.

Did you stick to your "no snacks/no pop" plan? Did you see any changes in your weight? Were there any extenuating circumstances during those two weeks? If you broke your foot and you're couchbound, this makes a difference. If you ran a marathon, this makes a difference. You get what I'm saying.

Act. Now you make a decision. Are you going to keep going on this weight loss plan because it seems to be working (even a little)? Or are you going to add in 20 minutes of exercise, and/or plan for one meal without carbs?

If all else fails, go back to the Plan step and review your problem. Be realistic in what problem you are trying to solve with your weight. There could be some underlying issues contributing to your outcome, or there may be additional data you haven't taken into consideration. (Ahem, ladies, it could not be a good "time" to try a weight loss routine, if you get my drift.)

Let's look at a process you could address at work. How about applying PDCA to that report your boss expects in her email box on Friday morning that takes forever to run?

Problem: The Friday Morning Report

Plan: Focus on the problem to solve, and start gathering your data. You could certainly say "The report takes too long to run, and I have to give it to her on Friday first thing in the morning." True statement, but it doesn't tell me what problem you are trying to solve! Ask specific questions.

What report? Does it have a name or specific content? What does "too long" mean? "Too long" could be five minutes or five hours!

You said you have to give the report to "her." Who is that? It is best to use her title, not her name, as you want to acquire data that will not change as new people step into positions.

Next, define "first thing in the morning." My day starts at 7 AM, but yours might start at 9 AM. "First thing in the morning" is a broad window, so you need to be specific.

Try writing out your problem like this: "Each week I complete a financial status report for the Manager of Accounting. It is due to the Manager every Friday at 8 AM. This process currently requires four hours to complete using an all manual process." Doesn't that make more sense? It tells me what problem we are trying to solve AND includes that baseline data we will need for our later comparisons.

Do: Now it's time to DO SOMETHING! Wave your magic wand, and *poof*...all better! Well, not quite, but close. Work with your team members to automate the report, and add in some error proofing. (I am sure you *never* made any errors in your manual process, but let's put that in there for good measure and to make sure that we can prove your report has the correct outcome.)

Check: Check your work! If you are trying to improve the speed to run a report, then yes, you can likely see right away if it is running faster. But you may need to ask other questions, also. Is the automation producing the report faster than when you did it manually? Does it require less than four hours to complete? Is it less manually intensive than before? Are there any errors in the report? Did you end up fixing something else in the process that you didn't even know was broken to begin with? If you are satisfied with the outcome of the Check step, then you are ready to take ACTION.

Act: Declare the new process for running the report! Update your instructions and documentation for this functioning report, and make that the solution to the problem (until you come back and make it even better later on). If the report isn't quite right and needs a little more "massaging," then go back to the Plan step to begin again. Perhaps you need to revisit the first step to ensure you really understand what's going on with that report today.[2]

Finally, let's look at an example for your home. (And for this, I'm using an actual story from *my home.*)

Problem: The White Stains on Katie's Black Pants

Plan: All of my black dress pants came out of the washer/dryer cycle with white stains on them, making them unsuitable for me to wear to work.

Do: Hubby believed the dryer sheets were causing the stains. In the next load of black dress pants we did not include a dryer sheet.

Check: Removed the load of pants from the dryer (without the dryer sheet) and reviewed. White stains were still there!

Act: We didn't fix the problem of the white stains, so we had to go back to the Plan step.

Plan (take two): We brainstormed a list of factors that could be causing the white stains. The stains started showing up in October, and what else may have changed then? Did the washing machine need to go through the "clean" cycle? What was my husband doing wrong? (Just kidding... maybe.)

Do: We recalled that we started using new baking soda based laundry detergent in October. We noticed that the rim around the detergent dispenser was also white, indicating a link between the cause and effect. I ran out and bought a new, green bottle of fresh smelling detergent that was not baking soda based.

Check: Hubby ran another load of black dress pants this time using the new detergent *and* a dryer sheet. No white stains!

Act: Problem solved, and decision made. We aren't going to use the baking soda based laundry detergent anymore, as it was the cause of the stains on my dress pants! Baking soda is white, and it wasn't dissolving during the wash cycle.

A process is *transformational* converting inputs into outputs. You follow and use processes every day, when you run that report, get ready for work in the morning, or pay your bills at the start of each month. What process in your life could use a little tweaking? Jump right in. You can use this space to get started.

Problem:	
Plan	
Do	
Check	
Act	

CHAPTER FOUR: TAKE OUT THE GARBAGE

Eliminate Waste from Your Life and your Processes

Right now picture your favorite gas station. Think of the one close to your home or your office, the one that you go to all the time.

In the space below write down all of the steps required to fill your vehicle with gas. Number each step from the moment you pull into the station, including pumping and paying for gas, and finally exiting the station. Perhaps you are thinking right now, "Wow, that's a lot of steps!" You're right. So let's get started.

Go.

I like to use this gas station example when I am working with a team, especially if they may not necessarily understand the complexity of a process and just how many steps are required to complete one of their routines. Honestly, I usually use this example with executives so they can understand the task from a 50 foot view instead of a 50,000 foot view. It can be highly effective to put them in the weeds.

At the end of the activity I facilitate a dialogue where we compare the number of steps on each person's list. On average most executives tell me they listed 16 steps, from pulling into the station, getting the fuel, paying for the gas, and leaving.

Then I tell them how many steps I have listed in my documentation of the same process.

Are you ready for this? *Forty-two.*

When we start to review and read aloud the steps from the individuals and teams we quickly find out that they skipped some crucial steps, like putting the car in park. Some of them forgot to include turning off the ignition. Others even neglected to take off their seatbelt! There is a LOT more to a process than meets the eye!

I encourage commentary as we review the steps, and one of the most consistent questions I hear is this one: "Why do you do it that way?"

Why do you lock your vehicle once you park it?

Why don't you have your credit card ready in your pocket when you get out of the van?

Why do you have to dump out your purse to find it?

Why do you do it that way?

This concept of the 5 Whys[8] encourages us to ask questions to identify the root cause of a problem and any opportunities there may be for improvement. Of course, two of the key factors to keep in mind are tone of voice and body language. The tendency might be to ask, with your mother's voice and inflection, "Why did you do it THAT way?" Instead, sometimes you have to channel the softer, kinder tone of your grandma and ask, "Can you help me to understand why you approached it like that?"

While it seems straight forward there are actually three different versions of any process:

1. The way that the process is documented, like in a standard operating procedure (SOP), work instruction, or directions on a website or box.
   Example: The illustrated instructions on the fuel pump at the gas station.
2. The way that you *think* the process works.
   Example: Your mental vision of yourself pumping gas into your car.
3. The way the process is *actually* done.
   Example: The lengthy, physical, pen to paper list of every single step required to complete the process.

As you might imagine each of these versions differs vastly from the others.

Here's are a couple of examples from the people I love: My dad is "follicly challenged." His normal routine is to get out of the shower, towel dry his hair, get dressed, and then put his small black comb in his back pocket. (You know, that one all the dads in their seventies and eighties carry in their back pocket.) Then he would go back to the bathroom, run the comb *through the WATER*, and comb his hair. Thirty years into their marriage Mom finally asked him about it. "Why do you do that with your hair? You dry it and then you WET a comb to style it. Why don't you just style it when it's wet?"

Honestly, he had never thought of doing it any other way. That was the way he had always done it, never taking a step back to see if there was a more efficient way to complete that process. Once Mom pointed it out to him, he agreed it seemed silly. This is what happens to most of us when someone objectively points out a blatant gap in a process, often an obvious opportunity for improvement to save you time (and often money). Once you can find those little nuggets you can hone in to fix them and eliminate the waste.

We have a couple of tractors in our barn, and with tractors come implements. HEAVY implements. These are not small tools that you can pick up and move by hand, and there never seems to be a good place to store them so they are out of the way when they are not in use. Constantly picking up and moving each implement to a different spot before we can access another, IS a waste of time. My hubby came up with a genius idea to eliminate most of the waste of both time and space: he visited a restoration hardware store, he bought some old doors, wood, and rolling casters, and he built platforms on wheels. Genius! Now we store the implements on the individual platforms, and we can wheel them all over the barn! We can move them close when we need them, and then roll them back when we are finished. It has saved a huge amount of time—and back pain!

We can often see the gaps in someone else's processes far before we can see our own.

Maybe you don't think there is anything to trim or tweak in your routines. But, with an average of 95% waste in any process, we are literally tripping over the excess in every process that we do, every single day. Are you having a hard time seeing the waste? Can't see what's extra? Just ask your partner. They can likely point it out to you. We can often see the gaps in someone else's processes far before we can see our own.

There are actually eight types of waste that are common in most processes, and we can remember them with the acronym **DOWNTIME**. The name itself should put a little anxiety in your heart. This isn't the good type of downtime, like when you go on vacation and have so much time on your hands. It's the other kind, like when the coach takes his best player out of the game because of an injury. Downtime is not a win.

Think of the downtime on the manufacturing floor as the team members work to do a changeover. Think of the downtime as the jury waits for the judge to reach a decision. Think of the downtime over the holiday break when the kids are home from school, and you have no idea what you are going to do with them. Downtime keeps us from moving forward.

The DOWNTIME acronym stands for: Defects, Overproduction, Waiting, Non-utilized talent, Transportation, Inventory, Motion, and Excess processing. Let's break them down, one at a time.

Defects. Plain and simple, this refers to the outcome that didn't turn out as expected, didn't meet your needs, or didn't satisfy your customer's requirements.

Recently I bought a fancy square muffin pan from a high-end cooking boutique that hosts cake decorating parties on a Tuesday night and prices even a spatula at $25.00. This new muffin pan was touted as "The Pan" to use for brownies and corn muffins. First time using it: corn muffins that were so burnt I had to use a knife to cut off the black parts, then put lots of butter on the remainder of the not-so-burnt parts just to drown out the taste of the burnt corn. That's a defect.

Another example is when you try to make a cute birthday cake for your kids hoping to save some money because you don't want to spend the hundred bucks on the bakery version; you believe you can create it based on the "inspiration" picture; and it comes out so horribly wrong that your mermaid cake looks like Jaba the Hut. That's a defect.

Overproduction. Overproduction is producing more than what is needed. Like when you intend to make spaghetti for two, but you end up with enough pasta to feed a family of 12. (You know you have done that.) Overproduction is leftovers in the fridge that have been there for an undetermined amount of time, but your husband asks if it is okay to eat them.

It is also making onboarding folders in advance for the whole year in anticipation of "expected" new hires. It is continuing to operate a machine because you still have raw materials left over from the original customer order. You start either making extras in anticipation of another order, or because you think it "costs too much" if you don't keep that machine running every minute of every day.

Waiting. Oh, hello, perhaps you are familiar with the Department of Motor Vehicles or Secretary of State in your area? No offense to them or other government offices, but how many countless hours of your life have you lost waiting in that place or waiting for someone to pick up the phone at the unemployment office?

Perhaps you've spent some time watching your computer screen, staring at "the spinning wheel of death," waiting for that report to run. You know what it's like to stand at the copy machine and wait for 100 copies of your presentation to finish printing or what it's like to wait for USPS to deliver the parts you need. You get it. You're no stranger to waiting.

Non-Utilized Talent. In my opinion this one is by far the worst version of waste. This one gets personal... it's about you. It refers to your missed opportunities to work to your full potential, either because you don't know what you're capable of, or because someone else doesn't recognize it. It's the most painful of errors.

Let's say you are on the IT team as a business analyst, and you are really good at making websites. You hear in a meeting that they are going to hire an outside contractor to update the company website, but you just can't muster up the courage to raise your hand to give it a try. You're too nervous to show them your portfolio, or no one ever asks if you have interest in doing this at work. That's non-utilized talent.

Or maybe your best friend decides to focus on physical fitness as a goal for the new year, and she never asks for your help (even though you have been friends for 100 years and you have been a certified fitness instructor for 10 of those years). This term refers to being overlooked or underutilized for new opportunities (even though the idea of doing it may leave you scared shitless).

Transportation. This aspect refers to the movement of goods, services, or information in a non-efficient manner. How many times do you walk into your kitchen or your office only to stand there absently because you can't remember why you came? Or, how often do you have to return to find something you forgot? How many more times are you going to move those boxes around your garage before you finally unpack from your recent move—two years ago?

Do you get frustrated emailing large files back and forth with your co-workers? It clogs up your email box, and you end up having to delete or archive other emails just to send a new version. If you place that presentation on a shared drive, internal website, or team application, you can more easily share it and keep track of revisions.

Inventory. This is about acquiring more than you would normally consume. (Hello, toilet paper hoarders of the world! I may or may not have a family member who is guilty of this habit.) Inventory costs money. The longer that an item sits on your (physical or virtual) shelf, the more it ends up costing you in the long run. You don't need more than you need.

Inventory issues can creep in when you find yourself buying five boxes of cereal instead of one. Let's be honest, they were on sale. But then they sit unopened on your pantry shelf until they expire, and you have to throw them out.

Inventory waste can also happen if you buy 5000 parts instead of the 500 you need to make your product. Or you might purchase an expensive software suite, even though you only ever use the word processing and spreadsheet software, and you leave the remaining apps unopened. (You may or may not have this installed on your computer right this minute.)

Motion. This encompasses bending, stretching, reaching, and grabbing... and I am not talking about Pilates or yoga. Consider the motion of picking up the toys from the family room floor every single night. Or how about getting on a chair, or, let's be honest, climbing on the counter, to find something on the top shelf like that turkey platter you use once a year.

I know of someone who walked onto a manufacturing floor only to find two people sitting on cardboard boxes instead of chairs or stools. That was a waste of motion, as they were trying to keep themselves balanced on the boxes without the right ergonomic support.

Remember we reviewed how to set up your desk in the 5S example? We talked about where to put your phone so you don't have to reach all the way across your desk to answer it. Yep, that's eliminating waste of motion too.

Excess Processing. Simply, excess processing is over-doing it. More sparkles, more shine, more of anything that doesn't really need to be done, only to make it "better" in your mind. It's your compulsion to redo your kid's project or your partner's presentation to make it "look" or "flow" better (especially if no one ASKED you to do that). It's shining that chrome on the new bike a little bit more before it comes off the line. It's giving me a presentation and a binder full of material when I only asked for a spreadsheet of the names of the people that took my Green Belt class last year. Excess processing includes any details that go above and beyond the actual deliverable. At the end of the day, it's a waste of time.

Why is it important to know the DOWNTIME wastes? Because when you recognize them, you can work to eliminate them! You want to get so good at recognizing the wastes in a process or situation that you can walk by and automatically think to yourself, "Look at all that waste. So much motion and excess processing." Or, "This process will work SO MUCH better if we can just eliminate the transportation of the paperwork from one desk to another." Waste is just an opportunity for improvement. It's the "easy" place to start to make a process or a place better, more organized, or more efficient.

Waste is more than the trash can at the end of the driveway on Monday mornings. Let's get rid of it, save you some time, and add more value to everything you do.

CHAPTER FIVE: SQUARE PEG IN A ROUND HOLE

Mistake Proofing

Have you updated your homeowners or auto insurance recently? Maybe you are looking to see if there are any other companies out there that can save you some money. Wow, now that's a process and experience that needs some improving. So many questions, so many options, bundled with some fear that you won't select the correct coverage, and then you'll get caught in a bad situation if/when your house burns down. (True story, it happened to us several years ago.)

Maybe you are trying to switch cell phone carriers, and you need to understand the coverage areas and what their "unlimited plan" *really* means.

You may be a new employee in a company, and now you need to figure out where and how to login to ALL these new systems.

Mistake Proofing is a system of checks and balances to reduce or eliminate the possibility of a mistake.

Don't you wish there was a "foolproof" way to do these things? There can be! The concept is called **Mistake Proofing**, a system of checks and balances that makes it impossible to put a square peg in a round hole. You create a system to reduce (or eliminate) the possibility of you (or someone else) making a mistake.

A major auto manufacturer conducted a study a few years back to determine the top reason that people came to the dealerships for service. They analyzed all of the data from all over the world, and they determined that the leading problem that brought people to get their vehicle serviced was the Check Engine light.

Remember, back in the day, when you had to turn the gas cap until you heard three "clicks" that indicated it was on tight enough? When your gas cap isn't tightened all the way it sends an error code to the vehicle. The Check Engine light goes on, and people drive to the dealership.

Been there, done that. I was newly single and driving to work. Halfway there, and about a mile from a dealership (thank God), my Check Engine light came on. I panicked. *Omg, what's wrong with my car?! What am I going to do? I don't have anyone to call if I break down on the highway!* Trigger: major anxiety.

I pulled into the dealership, and they brought me into the service bay right away. The service manager plugged their handy-dandy computer into my car to diagnose the problem, and then he walked to the back of my car, opened the gas door, and tightened the cap. Problem solved.

Talk about feeling dumb.

As a result of studying the not tightened gas cap, the auto manufacturer used the concept of mistake proofing to create the capless gas tank. The majority of the new vehicles produced today no longer have a cap on the gas tank. (This will give you quite the fright if you rent/buy a vehicle, don't see the cap, and automatically assume someone stole it!) This change has eliminated the number one reason why people (like me) came in for service, freeing time for both the drivers and the auto mechanics.

So, how can you create a situation where you can't make a mistake? Look closely at the process, and get ahead of the problem.

Do you keep running out of diapers, dog food, or deodorant? Mistake Proof it. Use the subscription feature from any of the major online retailers to automatically ship these items to your home every X-number of weeks, and you'll never run out again.

Are you tired of worrying about that compliance report, all the manual work in Excel, and whether or not you made a mistake? Mistake Proof it. Through automation and testing that report runs on its own with zero mistakes, and you are free to do more value added work.

Are you always missing an engagement, doctor's appointment, or kids' event? Mistake Proof it. Get into the habit of putting everything in your digital calendar, and set digital reminders. If you have an email address, then you have an online calendar associated with the account, and you have access to reminders. Set the reminder when you create your calendar event so you'll get an email reminder 15, 30 or 60 minutes before the event begins. As an added precaution for events I *really* don't want to miss, I also send an invite to my hubby. That way we both get the reminders of what is happening.

The credit card machine at the checkout of any store is an example of Mistake Proofing. There is (usually) a chip reader and a stripe reader, but the manufacturers want you to use the chip. So the machines are designed with mistake proofing; if you have a chip in your card, it won't let you swipe it!

Auto manufacturers are constantly coming up with ways to prevent you from locking your keys in your car, including features like beeping the horn or flashing the lights if you walk away without your keys.

Keep in mind, most of these solutions are low-to-no cost to you, and it just takes a little time to set them up and a little discipline to maintain them. Where are some areas of your life that can use a little Mistake Proofing?

Pause for a Confidence Break.

You might be thinking,

*"Katie, these are really great ideas,
but I don't have the confidence to believe
I can really make my life better
by improving absolutely anything."*

Yes, you can do this.

*Revisit the utensil drawer in your kitchen.
Look at the proof that you can adapt to systems of
organization and improvement.*

You can do (seemingly) hard things.

CHAPTER SIX: SEEING IS BELIEVING

Visual Management

Why does that utensil drawer organizer work for just about everyone on the planet? It works because it is easy to understand without words or instructions. In many organizers the spot for the forks is easy to identify because of the "saw" marks at the top of that space in the tray. The area for the knives is easy to identify because it's a long, narrow space in which the forks and the spoons wouldn't fit. The utensil drawer utilizes examples of Visual Management. We understand things when we can see them.

All over the world the universal sign for STOP is a red sign with white letters. It's the same with a stoplight; though the placement might be different, the red light always means STOP. We can speak different language and still understand the visual cues.

Some airports use visual management. When you are driving up the ramp to park at the airport some have signs that tell you how many open spots are at that level. Other parking areas even have lights hanging directly above the parking spots so you can easily see what is available, with a green light for vacant spots, and a red light for occupied spots.

Visual Management employs the art of making things easy to read, recognize and follow with few "written" instructions.

You don't have to read a manual to understand that the blue

bin with a "recycle symbol" on it is for recyclable material. You don't need written instructions to identify which bathroom to use, either the one with the symbol of a man or a woman. These are all examples of visual management, the concept that employs the art of making things easy to read, recognize, and follow with few "written" instructions.

You probably already do this improvement strategy without even knowing it. Do you have a luggage tag on your suitcases or backpack? Is there something flashy on that black piece of luggage that makes it easier to find on the conveyor belt? I bet your vehicle has a sticker that shows where you bought it and what about your state license plate that you customized with your favorite football team colors (which may be green and gold). That's visual management!

My favorite way to apply this concept is with my calendar and email. I use gmail, and all of my customer meetings on my calendar are in red because that helps me quickly see them in the sea of blue (default calendar color). The emails from my customer contact list automatically appear with a "star" on them in my Gmail inbox. I always have my calendar set to the workweek view, and I review it every Sunday evening and each morning during the week. By using the color coding technique I can quickly see how I need to prepare for each week at a glance, and I save time (and anxiety).

Anytime I travel I use a bright red, letter-sized plastic envelope with a Velcro closure, an item available online or at any office supply store near you. I place all of my travel documents, boarding passes, etc., in the red envelope before I set off on my adventures. This way I can reach into the vast cavern of my backpack to quickly find it, not only because it is red, but also because the slippery, plastic texture is different than anything else in my bag. I can literally reach into my bag and find it without looking, and this prevents me from fumbling around at the ticket gate trying to remember where I placed my boarding pass.

Sure, most boarding passes can now be delivered electronically, but what if you can't get reception inside the airport? What if your flight is delayed and your phone battery has died? Sometimes a hard copy is a good thing.

When I travel I put all of my receipts in that same red folder. At the end of the trip I have everything to log in my expenses when I get back home. This saves me the process of searching through pockets, bags, purses, and suitcases to find all of my receipts.

You can organize your closet with the concept of visual management. Like most of us, I have a designated area in my closet for pants, and I have three kinds of hanging pants: jeans, dress pants, and riding pants. That means my closet is a visual sea of blue, black, and (occasional) beige. I use visual management by regrouping my pants: jeans on the left, riding pants in the middle, and dress pants on the right. For additional visual cues I have tagged all of the hangers for my riding pants with a large neon pink label on the hanger. That way I can quickly see the "dividing line" between the sections, and I can easily grab what I need.

I even use visual management on my horses! They each wear a dog tag, and each saddle has a bright yellow luggage tag—just in case one of them decides that they might go on a "field trip" when I am on a trail ride. They each get grain every day from clearly labeled containers in the aisle cabinet, and each horse's food container is stored in a specifically shaped box (square or rectangle). Each container is labeled with the horse's name, "AM" for breakfast, and "PM" for dinner.

In our refrigerator, we have a designated shelf for leftovers. The second shelf on the right is the leftover shelf, and I even printed a label and placed it on that shelf. Each time we cook and have leftovers we place the containers on that shelf. Now there is no question what is available to eat!

How can you use visual management at work?

- Create signage that is easy to understand like the popular symbol for "mask required".
- Display some of your metrics on a TV with easy to understand visual indicators for good metrics (green) or bad metrics (red).

- Implement system notifications so, as soon as a user logs into a system, they will get an indicator of any required actions, like completing that required annual training… again.
- Create physical or electronic boards to indicate the status of a team member's work or an order.
- You can apply visual management to virtual sessions and video conferencing by adjusting your background. Do you want your audience to pay attention to you speaking on the screen, your presentation, or the messy room behind you?
- Convert your presentation slides to be more visually engaging rather than death by bullet points.

Important side note: be aware of any limitations that your audience or team members may have with color coding. True story: My team at corporate America was entirely colorblind. All of them! We had a standing joke that you couldn't be on my team unless you couldn't see color!

Most people are visual creatures by nature. Consider what visuals attract your attention. Why are you drawn to that image? Is it the color, the setting, the concept, or how it makes you feel? Apply those same concepts to how you work and live every day.

CHAPTER SEVEN: STARS AND BLACK MARKERS

Kanban Board

I remember when I was a little kid my mom created a homemade calendar to track my behavior. On the days when I was "good," I literally got a lick it and stick it gold star on the calendar. On the days that I most likely drove my mom nuts the date was colored in with a black marker. It hung in plain sight on the harvest gold refrigerator as an indicator of my behavior, though I'm not sure if it was displayed with pride...lots of black boxes for me! At a quick glance, anyone could see how I was doing, each day, week, and month.

The concept of kanban[9] (pronounced *kaan-baan,* not *can-ban*) provides a visual indicator regarding the status of something (like my three-year-old behavior patterns), or to indicate that something needs to happen.

Manufacturing facilities use kanban with signage to indicate when more parts are required on the line and sometimes an electronic signal to alert when assistance is required. It's kind of like a giant red flashing light (sometimes a *literal red flashing light*) to say, "Over here! I need something right now! Look at me! Look at me!"

In real life we can use kanban boards to indicate behavior or monitor progress on projects, team workload, and issues. We can use them at home to understand the status of chores, school work, behaviors, and "to do" lists.

Again, let's revisit the things that "bug" you the most. Are you struggling with keeping track of the tasks and status of your team now that most everyone is remote? How about staying organized with all of the assignments due for your three kids who are all remote learners? Tired of reminding the family to do their chores every single day? A kanban board would be the PERFECT solution for you!

As always we start out with low to no cost solutions for you. You need:

- A writing space big enough for at least three columns. Perhaps an old corkboard, a whiteboard, one of those extra large sticky note papers (2' x 3'), or even a blank piece of legal-sized paper would work.
- Sticky notes, file cards, or colored paper that you can write on.
- Draw columns wide enough to fit your file cards.
- Label the columns: *To Do, Doing,* and *Done.*

Let's say we are creating this kanban board for your kids' homework assignments. Each one of your kids gets a different color sticky note. Lilly has yellow, Brent has blue, and Sawyer has teal. Each week every child lists the assignments that are due on individual notecards, and they place them in the *To Do* column.

During the week, as they are physically working on their assignments, they then move the corresponding notecard from the *To Do* to the *Doing* column. As they finish, complete, or submit their work for that assignment they then move the card from the *Doing* column to the *Done* column.

You could have a quick family meeting every morning to review the status of the board and to help keep everyone on track. Something inside of us feels so satisfied when we move those notes from one stage to the next and especially when we move it to the Done column. At the end of the week celebrate their accomplishments. As we all know what is rewarded gets repeated, so make a big deal about it, people!

What is Rewarded gets Repeated.

My team and I used this concept to track the progress of the projects they were working on. We started out with a giant (I mean, *huge*) whiteboard on wheels, and we made our initial creation of the columns we thought we would use. As I mentioned above, we assigned a colored sticky note to each team member. We utilized the PDCA concept (imagine that!) to refine that manual board over the course of a month until we got it to a place that was workable for everyone. Then we converted it to an electronic version using a software tool we already had in house. Our board was displayed on a TV in the middle of our aisle, and we met each day for 15 minutes to go over the status of everyone's projects. We added a special column called "escalate," which was an indicator for me that someone needed help. I had 24 hours to help solve the issue, and if I couldn't solve it, I asked for help from my manager. Everyone could see the status of every task.

There are SO many ways that you could integrate this concept for yourself! You could create a kanban board for:

Paying bills (To Do, Paying and Done columns)
Household chores
IT coding projects
Agile (methodology) projects
Status of customer service tickets
Christmas gifts (Ideas, Ordered/Bought, Received)
Wedding/Event planning
Social media/marketing
Podcasts (Idea, Interview, Editing, Published)

The key to the success of a kanban board is two-fold: 1) follow the PDCA cycle to keep making it better until it works for you, and 2) remember the final S in the 5S tool, Sustain! Keep using it (just like your utensil drawer organizer) so you can reap the full benefits.

What benefits do you think you can glean from using this

super easy, low cost, visual tool? It gives you a great overall look at a process. Whether you're focusing on homework assignments, Christmas gifts, or social media posts, you can see the status of everything at one glance with little room for interpretation. It's either in progress or done (not done-done), there is no in-between. It helps you to understand your kids' workload and your team members' workload (should Sammy really be slacking off this week?), and it helps you to improve absolutely anything.

When you create a kanban board you are not only solving a problem for you, but believe it or not, you are also helping your internal and external "customers." A kanban board at work will help your team members keep track of their projects and provide an easy way to ask for help. If you make a kanban board for homework, first you'll keep from losing your ever-loving mind, *but also* your kids and their teachers will benefit. That's the beauty of improvement: it benefits more than one person.

Start thinking about how these concepts may help you, as well as those around you. Who else benefits when the family vehicle is organized? Is anyone else happy that their black pants and dark clothes don't come out of the washer with stains on them? What other person(s) would appreciate it when you don't miss their meeting (again)?

CHAPTER EIGHT: IT'S NOT ALL ABOUT YOU

The SIPOC Tool

Have you ever been in a situation when—*oops!*—you forgot to invite someone to a party or a meeting? Maybe you made a change with the pickup routine for your kids, but you forgot to tell the school? Perhaps you changed a process at work to the way you *thought* would be better, but—*eek!*—you actually made your co-workers' job harder as a result?

When we are trying hard to make improvements we can get so excited and caught up in the moment that we might forget to look outside our own bubble to discover that others may be impacted, both positively or negatively.

Remember that manual report that you were working on fixing when we spoke about PDCA? You went through all of the steps, automated it, added in error checking, and now it is electronically delivered to your boss on time every week. What you might not have thought about was the fact that the information in that report is used by your boss to analyze and summarize to then send to the CEO. The new format you created during the automation process sends your boss a PDF report (and we all know you can't do much with a PDF!). The way you used to complete the report provided the document to your boss in Excel. Though you were trying to be more efficient you actually forgot to ask your boss what she needs in order to do her job!

Maybe you created that awesome kanban board for work. Your

team was using it every day. It was awesome! You decided to make an electronic version of it, but you forgot that a couple of your team members don't have access to that system. Or, maybe a few of your team members are colorblind, and they can't see all of the neat color-coding indicators on a virtual board.

True story: We get mail order prescription medications at our house, and the delivery arrives a few days before we are supposed to run out of our medicines. When my hubby received the new prescription bottle, he would pour its contents into the "old" bottle with the remaining pills. Then he would throw out the "new" bottle (that is now empty). Seems like a fairly meaningless task, right? Yes, until we could no longer determine how many refills he had left on his medicine. The new labels were thrown out with the new bottles leaving us only with the original label on the original bottle. (This was before online refills were a thing.) Some of those old bottles were years old prescribed by doctors he no longer saw. (That shows how long he had been doing that process!)

The same applies when other people are trying to implement concepts or processes for improvement, and they accidentally negatively impact you. For example, after reviewing a year's worth of data of their customer flow, the local dealership decides to change their hours for the quick lube station. They now stay open late one day a week, and they no longer have hours on Saturday. It might be an improvement for them, but the night they are open late is the same evening that your child has gymnastics. You work during the day leaving no possibility for you to take your car in. Ugh.

How about this: your partner decided to "organize" your kitchen pantry over the weekend (maybe even when you went away on a business trip or visit to your parents). Your partner is *so* proud, delighted to show you all the things that have been improved. Then they leave for work on Monday morning while you are getting the kids ready for school. You start the breakfast routine, and you open the pantry to get the kids cereal for breakfast. Your partner moved the Cocoa Puffs to the top shelf, but you can't reach that high without standing on a chair. *Oops*. Good intentions, but your partner didn't think about anyone else in the house who requires easy access to those Cocoa Puffs!

How can you prevent and overcome these situations? Use the SIPOC tool! SIPOC provides you with an overarching view of a process, and it allows you to see who might be impacted by a change. My teams typically create the SIPOC tool on a white board (physical or virtual), or on a blank page in a presentation software. The goal is not about being pretty, but it's about getting the task done to serve its purpose. On average these should take less than 30 minutes to complete.

SIPOC stands for Suppliers, Inputs, Process, Outputs, and Customers.[10]

S	I	P	O	C

Contrary to how we read words on a page (from left to right), we start a SIPOC directly in the middle: with the P for Process.[3]

Process. This step grounds us in the knowledge of what we are here to discuss. Think of it like a teeter-totter (or fulcrum): the Process is the pivotal point required for the tool to work.

Remember, a process is a method that transforms inputs into outputs. To begin the SIPOC tool, we want to describe our process at a VERY high level—only five to seven steps. Think of how you would describe a process to your partner, friends, or parents: keep it simple.

If you are describing the process you follow to make breakfast, you won't describe how you open the utensil drawer, pull out the spoon, place it on the counter, close the drawer, and on and on and on. No, you might say that you grab a spoon, get a cereal bowl, and sit down at the table. This is not a time to examine the opportunities in each step of your process. Just give an overview to get high level understanding.

If you can't describe your process in five to seven steps, then you might be trying to boil the ocean (tackling too big of a process). Scale it back.

Let's consider the process of feeding the dog:

1) Get the dog bowl
2) Open the pantry
3) Fill the bowl
4) Call the dog (Well, let's be real here... you don't have to call most dogs to eat!)

If we were running a pizza place, our pizza process might look like this:

1) Receive the order
2) Prepare the dough
3) Add sauce
4) Add toppings
5) Bake in the oven
6) Remove from the oven
7) Serve

Notice in the pizza example, I didn't include steps like, "Answer the phone to talk to the customer," or "Enter the order into the computer system." I also didn't include going to the refrigerator to get the dough, or tossing the dough in the air to make your pizza pie. We are operating from a high level here, people. The nitty gritty details are for another tool.

Now that we have our high level process, the P step is complete, and you move on to the O.

Outputs. What comes *out* of each step of the process? What is produced? What do we get? These are the outputs, and they can be physical or virtual, including actions and outcomes.

For feeding the dog, the Outputs would be:

1) Dog eats
2) Dog "fertilizes garden" (You get it... stuff happens.)

For our pizza place, the Outputs would be:

1) A perfectly baked pizza (am I making you hungry yet?)
2) A completed order
3) Dirty dishes

Now we move on to the letter C.

Customers. This category includes anyone—person, entity, company, etc.—that *consumes* your outputs. Your customers are the people who buy your product or service, or anyone impacted by your process.

Remember to think past the first person who will receive your work. You may give it to your boss, but they will also share it with the CEO of the company. You might manufacture parts and sell them to Company X, but if the government has hired them to produce the final product, then the government is also your customer.

For feeding the dog, the Customers would be:

1) Dog
2) Family
3) Garden

For the pizza example, the Customers would be:

1) Dine-In customers
2) Carry-Out customers
3) Delivery customers

We have completed POC, and now it's time for I and S, inputs and suppliers.

Inputs. Let's talk about inputs first. Inputs are everything required to successfully complete your product or outcome for your customers. It can be physical materials as well as virtual information, like a kanban signal or an online order. It could even be a person! We certainly need the chef in order to complete the custom dinner menu.

For feeding the dog, the Inputs would be:

1) Dog food
2) Hungry dog
3) Empty bowl
4) Specific time (i.e., maybe you feed your dog every day at 5 PM)
5) Human dog feeder (let's face it...it's normally mom)

For the pizza example, the Inputs would be:

1) Customer order
2) Dough
3) Spices
4) Toppings
5) Cheese
6) Oil (for the pan)

Finally, let's review the S (suppliers).

Suppliers. These are the people who help to kick off the process. The people, companies, agencies, etc., that supply your inputs. Our suppliers might include the grocery store where you buy your bananas, the vendor where you get your nuts and bolts, the government that funds the project, your kid's school district who hires and dispatches the bus drivers to transport your kids to school on time—even *you,* the one who feeds the dog.

For feeding the dog, the Suppliers would be:

1) The grocery store (Publix - the BEST grocery store EVER)

2) You (without you none of this is possible)

For making that beautiful, warm, and cheesy delectable pizza, the Suppliers are:

1) Veggie Farmers United
2) Sysco
3) Lamers Dairy (Hello, my fellow Wisconsinites!)

When we put it all together we have a fantastic, thorough, overall view of our process, whom it impacts and what we need to get it done!

Feed the Dog SIPOC

Suppliers	Inputs	Process	Outputs	Customers
Grocery store	Dog food	Get the dog bowl	Dog eats	Dog
You (the owner)	Hungry dog	Open the pantry	Dog "fertilizes garden"	Family
	Empty bowl	Fill the bowl		Garden
	Specific time	Call the dog		
	Human dog feeder			

Make the Pizza SIPOC

Suppliers	Inputs	Process	Outputs	Customers
Veggie Farmers United	Order	Receive order	A perfectly baked pizza	Dine-In customers
Sysco	Dough	Prepare dough	A completed order	Carry-Out customers
Lamers Dairy	Spices	Add sauce	Dirty dishes	Delivery customers
	Toppings	Add toppings		
	Cheese	Bake in the oven		
	Oil	Remove from the oven		
		Serve		

Perhaps now you can also see why it is important to start with the P (Process step). If we first asked, "Who are the suppliers?" we would have so many questions: Suppliers of what, for what? If we don't know the process we are talking about, then it would be very hard to complete the rest of the steps.

Remember, SIPOC=POCIS (or as my friend pronounces it, "pocus").

When I work with a team to create a SIPOC for a process we are trying to improve I hear this type of feedback:

"Wow, I had NO idea my step in the process impacted
this department or that person."
"I didn't realize that when I went to change that
step I had to tell someone else about it."
"I just assumed that we didn't need it for XYZ."
"I didn't know that the customer saw that!"

What would a SIPOC look like for your current process? Can you do a SIPOC for the way you manage your kid's homework assignments? How about a SIPOC for how you make dinner or bake cookies? Would yours look like mine? Yours will probably be different, and that's okay. That's the beauty of continuous improvement on a personal level.

Create a SIPOC for one of your processes. (Just give it a try.) Reflect on your process to see what you may have been missing when you were looking at it through a smaller lens. Then I want you to take a look at it to identify where you are doing a great job and where you can improve. Where are your strengths, and where are your weaknesses? Is there a trend?

CHAPTER NINE: EVEN WONDER WOMAN HAS A WEAKNESS

SWOT Analysis

If you are currently employed, then you have the "pleasure" of analyzing your strengths and weaknesses every year during the annual review process. Let's be honest. It's hard to think about how much you suck, and it's even harder to reframe that as more of an opportunity than an actual weakness.

If you aren't currently involved in the fun of the annual review process, I would still bet you have someone in your life willing to help you identify your weaknesses. That helpful voice might even be your inner critic. There is a tool we can use to balance this all out and put things into perspective. Whether we are looking at our personal skill set, or one of our processes, we can use a tool called a SWOT Analysis.[11]

SWOT falls into the "visual management" category, so this tool appeals to those of us who like to see things on paper, either physically or virtually. What is your preferred learning style? Visual learners learn by watching; auditory learners learn by listening; kinesthetic learners learn by working it out with their hands. Many of us are a mix of learning styles, and we usually lean toward the visual side of things.

Ever since I was a young person learning how to drive using navigational directions (turn East on Maple Ln and West on Klais) have meant very little to me. Then and today my version of directions sounds like, "Turn right at the green building, and then turn left at the red barn." If you try to tell me to go east, I will have absolutely no idea which direction you are talking about. I am not directionally challenged, but I work off of landmarks and unique identifiers. I am a visual learner and processor, and the SWOT works well for people like me.

SWOT stands for Strengths, Weaknesses, Opportunities and Threats.

It is usually arranged like this on a graph:

Strengths	Weaknesses
Opportunities	**Threats**

Strengths. Strengths are things that you do REALLY well such as the skills that you brag about and the talents you are most proud of. They are also the details that give you a competitive edge, a one-of-a-kind offering, or what your customer likes the most about your product. This is what keeps them coming back for more. Another way to approach a strength is to consider how you are unique and what others view as your strengths.

Personal strengths might include: I am creative, I am a certified teacher, I reached my goal weight. Business strengths might include: We have 99% on-time delivery, we are operating at a 6 sigma level of quality, we have a 5-star rating on Facebook.

Reflecting on these items should offer a sense of pride for yourself (and your team). Begin by listing these in the Strengths box.

Weaknesses. Weaknesses are gaps in your skill set, areas where you don't perform well, and zones where you could improve—or where your customer believes you can improve. It's your kryptonite. This reflects a particular area where you could really utilize more resources (e.g., more tellers working in a bank, a full-time receptionist at your office, or a virtual assistant to manage your email and messenger responses).

You need to be realistic for this section. The pendulum usually swings one way or the other: either people are overly realistic about their weaknesses, or they are not. In my career, I have only received one annual review where someone listed their weaknesses as "None." (I seriously almost fell out of my chair when I saw that. I considered penciling in the space: Arrogance and Ignorance.) You and your processes have weaknesses. Be realistic, acknowledge them, write them down, and move on.

Opportunities. We don't have problems; we have opportunities for greatness. Opportunities are trends that you could take advantage of, certifications your team could obtain to raise their knowledge, and even job opportunities like shadowing and/or internships. Personal opportunities could include taking an online fitness class during your lunch break to help you reach your health goal, reading a highly recommended book on budgeting, or joining a LinkedIn group of people with similar interests. Professional opportunities might include looking into new technology that makes it easier for people to work remotely, improving your website's processes based on customer feedback to make checkout smoother (like accepting Amazon pay), or joining the local small business association as a learning and networking opportunity.

Threats. Sounds ominous, doesn't it? Threats are anything that can harm you, your company, your innovations, your IP. A threat is the Joker to your Batman. Threats can include details like a change in your work schedule, from first shift to third shift, that interferes with your ability to continue your education or childcare. Perhaps a sudden, unprecedented demand for your online tool can be a threat, if you don't have the capacity to meet demand. A threat can also be a health concern. If you are struggling to keep a health condition under control, it can become a threat to your well-being, your ability to work, and your family. Finally, check out your competition—worthy rivals are always a threat!

Wow. That's a lot to consider. Completing a SWOT Analysis can be a bit of an emotional journey, but that's not a bad thing. Get it all down on paper, be realistic in each category, and then you can start to digest it.

Please note: a SWOT is not a life evaluation tool. Don't create a SWOT to analyze everything that is "wrong" with you, how your partner irritates you, or the wicked behavior of your parents. Do not create a SWOT to evaluate a person or a relationship.

Create a SWOT with a cross functional team for your company quoting process. Create a SWOT for accepting a new patient into your medical practice. Even create a SWOT when you want to analyze your ability to finish your college degree or even obtain a professional certification. The intention is to acknowledge what is currently happening, to take your blinders off and discover factors that could impact you (now and in the future), and to determine an informed action plan to move forward.

Don't let your weaknesses consume all of your attention. Acknowledge each section of the SWOT analysis and move on. Don't try to boil the ocean. You are not going to solve all of your weaknesses in a week, a day, or a month. You certainly are not going to be able to fend off all your threats with one mighty swing of your magic lasso. (Remember, Wonder Woman had one!)

Let's take a look at a SWOT example for someone that wants to go back to school to get their master's degree through an online program.

Strengths Technologically savvy Good at communicating Familiar with school's online platform Required courses are topics I want to learn Quick learner Not much studying required (for undergrad)	**Weaknesses** Difficulty multitasking Waits until the last minute to complete tasks 12 years since the last college course
Opportunities Accelerated version of this program available (complete in 14 months vs 2 years) Employer will pay for 100% of the degree Courses completed at your own pace	**Threats** Current job role is demanding 50+ hour work week 2 kids virtual learning Partner is considering a new job that may require relocation

Based on this SWOT, what would you do?

I bet you are thinking, "Okay, so this person knows how to follow the 'rules' and create a SWOT like Katie described above. Now what?" Well, if this were me and my SWOT, I would use this graph to aid my decision-making process, and I would review each section.

Looking at strengths, I would think, I know I can do this! School comes really easy to me. My coworker Tina recently completed this same course work, so I have seen the materials already, and I know they utilize the same platform for the courses that I completed before. Therefore, I'm familiar with that as well. At this point I am feeling pretty pumped.

Now for the weaknesses...Ugh. Yes, sometimes I am scatterbrained by having too many things going on at once, and I rarely finish any of them. I do better with one task at a time. Yes, I tend to wait until the last minute to complete things, but I am taking a Lean course at work, and I have picked up a few tricks that I think are going to help me. Yes, it's been a while since I was in college, but I have taken other courses for certifications required for my job, so I know my brain isn't that stale.

Looking at opportunities gets me even more jazzed. An accelerated program might just be the ticket! Then it won't seem like it is drawn out forever, and the pace can motivate me to get my homework done on time. Plus, my employer will pay for ALL of my courses if I get an A or B. Talk about inspiration! That will save me $50K! I can also take these courses at my own pace, which could be a great thing for me (if I don't slack off).

I think I can do this, but there are a few threats to consider. My current role is a beast. I work *A LOT*. But, I also haven't voiced this to my boss, and she probably doesn't really realize how much time I work outside of "normal hours." I have an opportunity to explain this. My desire to get this degree and to continue to develop my skills will benefit the company (and me, let's be real) in the long run. Now that it has almost been a year, the kids have pretty much settled into a routine with their online learning. And, really, who knows if that will continue? My partner has a *potential* lead for a new role that *potentially* could require us to move. That's a lot of *potentials*, a lot of *ifs*. I already work from home, so *if* this would *actually* happen, I don't anticipate it being a problem for my employer.

What would you conclude if you walked through the SWOT analysis this way? The conclusion seems to point to: Go back to school! See how the SWOT assists with the heavy lifting of decision making? We use the SWOT to lay it all out there, to acknowledge, to be realistic, and to think logically through a process.

In my experience, there are not too many weaknesses and threats that can't be overcome if you apply your strengths and leverage your opportunities.

Now let's look at a SWOT for a work situation. Let's say you belong to a CPA firm that is on the cusp of a potential expansion. Your client base continues to grow year after year, and you now need to decide whether to hire an additional CPA for your firm so you can continue to grow.

Strengths	**Weaknesses**
25% client growth over the last 2 years. Viewed as the "go to" CPA for all of the members of the local chamber of commerce. Won the Best of 2020 for CPAs in our area. No audits for us or any of our customers over the last 10 years.	We are starting to have more work than we can handle. Our previous turnaround time for personal taxes was 3 days, now it's 14 days. We don't have an online presence. All paperwork has to be physically dropped off at our office or mailed to us. We work out of our homes.
Opportunities	**Threats**
We have had an intern working for us for the past 3 years, and she is about to sit for her CPA exam. There is a prime office location available downtown, and we would get a discounted rate because they are our clients. If we hired someone new and rebalanced the workload, we could conceptually serve our current and potential new customers for the next 10 years.	We will start having to turn people away if we don't make a decision soon (and potentially ruin our reputation). It's not secure to have our clients' actual paperwork at our current office space in our house. Another "big name" CPA firm has moved into the area—they have an online presence, and they charge less than we do.

Based on this SWOT, what would you do?

If the decision were mine, I wouldn't necessarily be too quick to hire a new CPA. There are a few things that I would suggest working through first.

I would investigate what changed in the process so we now require 14 days to complete a personal return. I would survey my customers to determine if they would prefer to upload their tax information to a "portal" rather than drop off the paperwork. I would consider the reality that sometimes technology can take the personal "touch" out of a relationship. I would also evaluate if working from home is really productive. Are there too many distractions? Is there enough room for work space vs living space, or is it all combined in one? If you hire a new CPA, is your previous intern the best person for the job? Why can't you rebalance the workload now to see if you can improve results, rather than just add another person into the mix? (Sometimes this seems to be an easy way to solve the problem, by just throwing people at it.)

What does that new CPA firm have that you don't have? (Besides money... they probably have more money.)

Does the SWOT analysis "speak" to you?

What's going on in your life right now that could benefit from a SWOT analysis?

New job? Career change? Broken process at work?

Can you create a SWOT analysis to help you make a decision?

~ ~ ~

If you know your learning style (and the learning styles of your team members and even your family), you can learn to communicate in the appropriate "language." There are several cool tools you can use to facilitate these conversations. Grab your colored markers (extra points if you use the scented ones that smell good), and let's go!

CHAPTER TEN: MY BRAIN IS ABOUT TO EXPLODE

Brainstorming

Do you ever feel like your brain is about to explode because there is SO much information in there, and if you don't get it out on paper, you are going to lose all of it? That happens to me. If I don't get my ideas out of my head, documented somehow and somewhere, it seems to "leak" out over time, disappear bit by bit in as little as a day or even an hour. This happens despite my best intentions, even though I often convince myself that I will "always" remember that information.

Maybe you received a new assignment at work, and you have a rush of ideas right away. Your brain is probably going faster than your mouth, and likely faster than your hand to document your great ideas.

Or maybe your team is facing a problem to solve, and you want to host a brainstorming session to get all of these great ideas out of people's heads and onto a white board.

One brainstorming tool that you can use is a **mind map**.[12] A mind map speaks to my fellow visual learners, but it also works well in communicating with the audible and kinesthetic folks, too. The idea behind a mind map is to use colors and images to brainstorm on a topic or to help solve a problem. At the end, you have an artistic type rendering of your brainstorming session, and it will likely look similar to the cartoon type depictions of your brain, with all of the off-shoots to the various parts of your body.

This is how it works: First, identify the problem you are trying to solve or the topic you want to brainstorm.

What's on the top of mind for you lately? Work situations? Home improvements? Virtual learning? Continuing education?

You can brainstorm on paper, a whiteboard, or on a virtually platform using an online brainstorming tool. If you are brainstorming in person, set up a whiteboard and some dry erase markers, or get a large piece of paper, a collection of colored markers, pens, and even crayons if you'd like. If you don't have colored markers, crayons, etc., no worries. Just use what you have.

In the center of your paper draw a circle This is your center point, the hub to your wheel. This is where ideas will "radiate" from. You can also think of this as the trunk of a tree.

Just for fun let's brainstorm ideas for your family vacation this year. Start with this in the center:

Now the fun and brain dumping begins! With your family members, your teammates for this project, take turns writing down ideas about the topic. The ideas will appear as extensions off your center idea, like spokes on a bicycle wheel or branches on a tree. Use different colors, create little drawings, and make it yours. Make sure that everyone has a "turn" to write out their ideas on the mind map. This tool allows you to get all of those fabulous ideas out on paper. By using the creative techniques of colors and images, it also helps you to remember what was discussed and to spark new ideas.

Your family vacation brainstorming map could look like this when you are done.

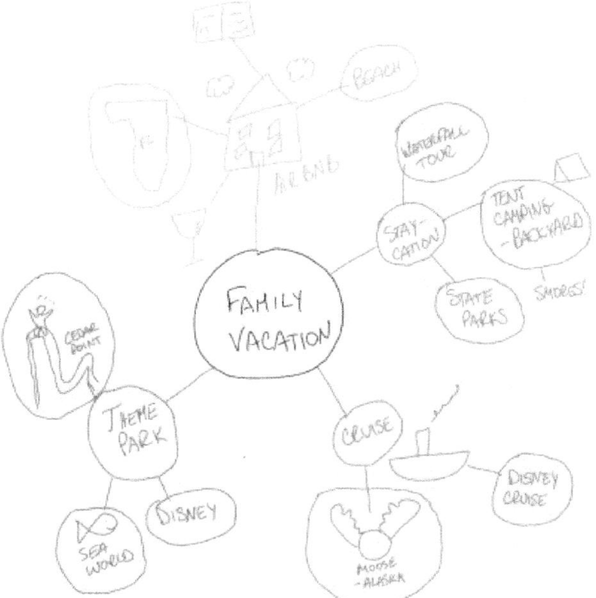

Now that you have all of your ideas written down, it's time to narrow down your scope. What do you want to focus on first?

Or, in this case, with our family vacation, how much money (and time) can we spend on vacation this year? If we need to be a little more cost-conscious, we can shift our focus to the "Staycation" section. We will review those ideas, add any more that might come up, and start creating a game plan for vacation this year.

What would this look like for a work situation? Not much different! Begin with the idea or problem you are trying to solve as your center point, and let your ideas "radiate" from there. If you brainstorm ways to make meetings more effective, your mind map might look like this:

If I were working with my team on this mind map, I would then lead the group to pick two or three areas to tackle first. These areas would be the ones that could really "move the needle" toward making their meetings more effective, or have the greatest "bang for the buck." Once we have investigated those areas and taken action the team should return to this original mind map for additional ideas, or even to update or add to it based on the information they gathered. The mind map is a living tool and a great resource for ideas!

There are several things to consider when creating a mind map:

- There can be NO criticism of ideas. (That's truly a good rule for really any brainstorming activity). As soon as the monster of criticism rears its ugly head the ideas stop flowing. People start to concentrate instead on defending their ideas and worrying if their thoughts are "good enough." Don't limit or restrict your ideas, and don't self-criticize either. No idea is a dumb idea unless someone gives it that label, either verbally or in your head. Don't let that happen.
- You can absolutely create a mind map yourself, but depending on the subject, a cross functional group of people will give you the best results.
- If you are in a virtual setting, you can use tools like Teams, Miro, or Mural to create a mind map on a virtual whiteboard.
- Know your audience. Some people would consider this group activity to be absolute torture. (You know who you are! Introverts, unite!). I have many years of experience in IT, and I majored in Management Information Systems in college. I can tell you this: this tool might not resonate with your IT team because different colors, symbols, and communicating in front of a group would not appeal to them. However, many HR groups LOVE this tool, as it speaks to their strengths.
- Know the culture of the team, company, and even geographic location. In some areas of the world the process of personally writing out ideas like these (especially some that could be viewed as controversial) would not be accepted, and no one would want to participate.

We make decisions all day, every day, for our work and home

lives. Pick one of those decisions or topics, and create a quick mind map for it.

CHAPTER ELEVEN: I HAVE AN AFFINITY FOR STICKY NOTES

Affinity Diagram

When I was studying for my Lean Six Sigma Black Belt exam there was SO MUCH material to remember. As many of us know, after studying hard for a long period of time the Law of Diminishing Returns[13] starts to slow us down. You can study your brains out, eight hours a day for a whole week, but you will actually retain only about 25% of the material (or even less).[14] The one tool that I had such a hard time remembering was the Affinity Diagram, so I created a little memory device to anchor it in my mind: "I have an affinity for sticky notes."

Yes, in my mind, the Affinity Diagram is The Sticky Note tool. It is another great brainstorming tool that you can use to come up with ideas on a topic or a problem. We use this tool when we have a lot of ideas, and/or those ideas appear to be floating all over the place in chaos. The Affinity Diagram can be used with a variety of teams, but it is an especially fabulous tool for that quieter, more introverted group of people who may not talk much, and *definitely* don't want to speak up in the group of their peers. You can create an Affinity Diagram, in person or virtual, using the online tools I noted in the previous chapter.

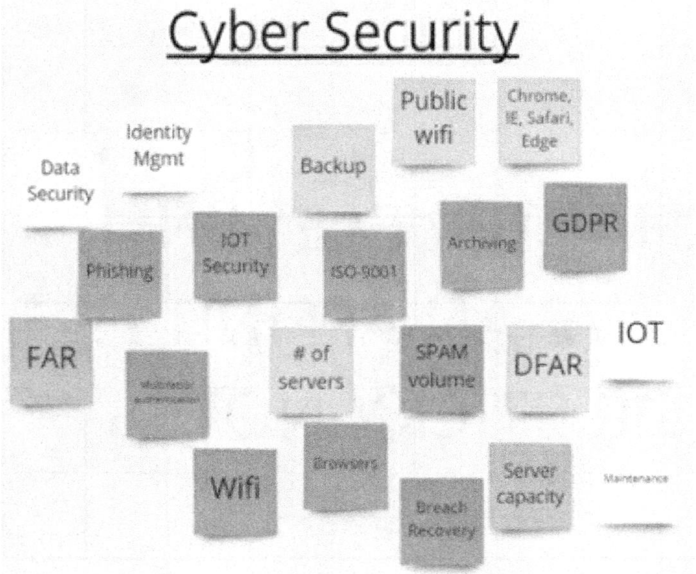

Begin with a topic to brainstorm or problem to solve. For an in person affinity diagram all you need are packages of sticky notes and pens for each person in attendance. Again, a cross functional group of people is a perfect team to contribute a variety of ideas. Usually, 8-10 people make a perfect group for this fun event.

Just like the mind map, you can use an affinity diagram for a topic at work or at home, dealing with any idea or problem you are trying to solve. Both the affinity diagram and the mind map can be completed in less than 30 minutes, depending on the topic, and both offer an outlet to those creative ideas floating around your mind that you need to get down on "paper."

For our example, let's explore a work topic: cyber security. Let's imagine our team wants to enhance the cyber security for our company, and we want to understand how to do this and what we need to consider.

Begin by simply listing our topic on the top of our white board or screen to make sure that everyone knows the focus of this activity. Now the brainstorming begins. On the sticky notes each person writes down their ideas, one idea per sticky note. When I facilitate one of these sessions I usually tell the participants that they have to come up with at least three unique ideas, and this guideline always leads to more once they get warmed up.

When everyone has written their ideas on the sticky notes they each post them to the white board. It can look like a giant mess of sticky notes, and that's exactly what we want to see. Remember: no criticizing ideas! It is actually a good sign if you see multiple sticky notes with the same idea!

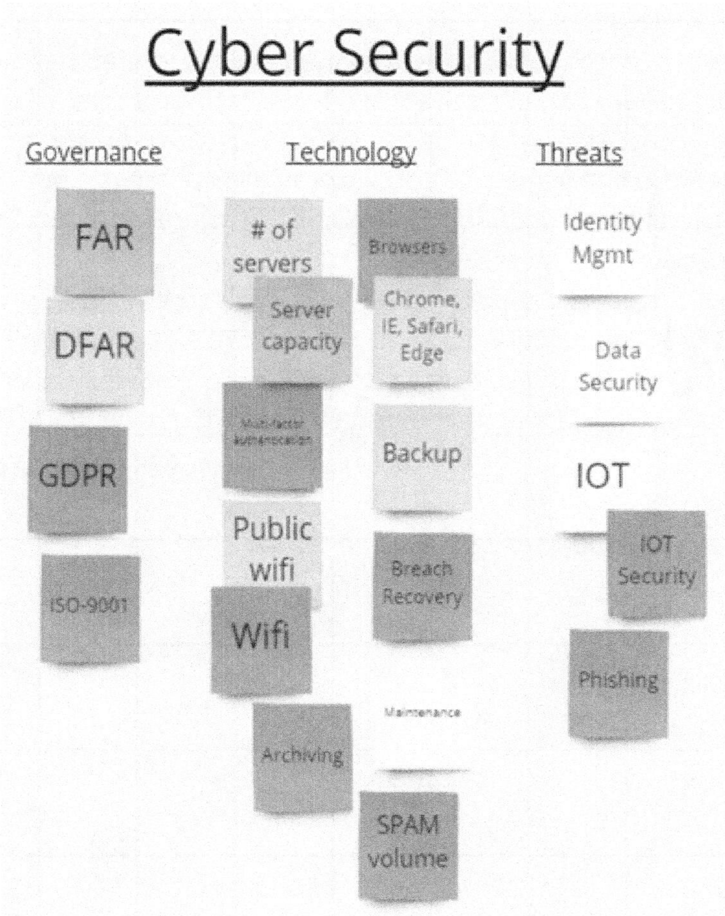

Next, you organize all of the sticky notes into columns based on their similarities. Create a label for each column of information you created.

Beware of the "Other" column. Try not to have a column of sticky notes that are labeled "Other." It won't help to solve your problem or come up with any creative solutions. Make sure every sticky has a home.

If you are using the affinity diagram to come up with solutions to the problem, what's your next step? It's not super scientific: if you want to know where to focus your time and effort first, look at your column with the most sticky notes! In our cyber security example we decided to investigate technology first. After you have looked into the technology surrounding cyber security, now look into the threats.

When you're creating an affinity diagram no "cheating" is allowed. In other words, don't start with predefined categories on your affinity diagram. Let the ideas come naturally based on the suggestions from the group. (If you want more structure, hang on, we have another tool for that.) This is a living document, and you can update and revisit it as needed.

For a more personal example, let's go back to the family vacation mind map where we decided to explore a staycation that involves going to one of the state parks that has a beach. Based on our family vacation affinity we need to first work on the Destination.

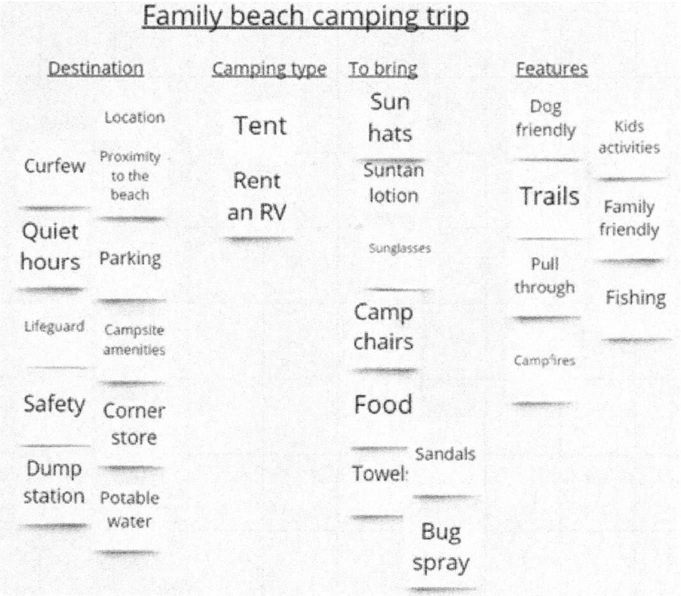

In this example, even though the Camping Type column has

only two sticky notes, it is important to consider this element when determining the destination, as your choice will dictate the type of camping, and vice versa.

Now that you know how to do both a mind map and an affinity diagram, go back to that “thing” that “bugs" you the most. Explore both the mind map and the affinity diagram to see what works best for you, and you’ll have a solution in your hands.

CHAPTER TWELVE: FISHY FISHY IN A BROOK

Fishbone Diagram

Let's go fishing for another tool! Do you like structure, but not too much? Maybe you feel comfortable following directions, but you also like to do your thing? You prefer an open parking lot with lots of choices rather than parking in a field at the fairground, and trying to line up with the cars all around you when nobody has lines to guide them. You hang some of your clothing on hangers, but you have your own system for the ones that are "supposed to be hung up," like sweatshirts: you fold them nicely and put them a drawer. Does this sound like you?

You are going to LOVE using a fishbone diagram if you thought, "Yes, that's me!"

(If not, then please, just humor me and read on.)

The Fishbone diagram is half-way between the mind map and the affinity diagram for those who need a little more structure and find comfort with a little more direction when dumping out your brains. Remember when we discussed how people learn and the preferences of your family/team? This appeals to the people in the middle. They like to be creative, however, they need a little bit of structure to help spark their ideas.

A fishbone diagram (also called an Ishiwaka diagram, or a Cause and Effect diagram)[15] is a structured brainstorming tool.

A fishbone allows you to dump your ideas, like a mind map, but it provides structure with already named categories (unlike the affinity diagram).

And guess what! The format of this tool is in the shape of a fish. (Imagine that!)

The fishbone diagram is straightforward and easy to use. It's a visual tool that involves a team to brainstorm ideas on a situation or a problem, and we have to begin by understanding the problem we are trying to solve or the topic we are there to discuss.

Let's start with a simple example. Pretend you own a coffee shop, and you have started to review your coffee sales. Here is the problem statement you created:

Our regular coffee has had the lowest sales of all of our coffees for the last six months. Customer feedback gives us a 1 star rating out of 5 stars. We need to increase sales and quality for regular coffee, as it is our highest margin product.

Start by drawing the diagram on a whiteboard or big piece of paper. Bring in your team members to help brainstorm ways to fix this problem.

Remember, no idea is a bad idea.

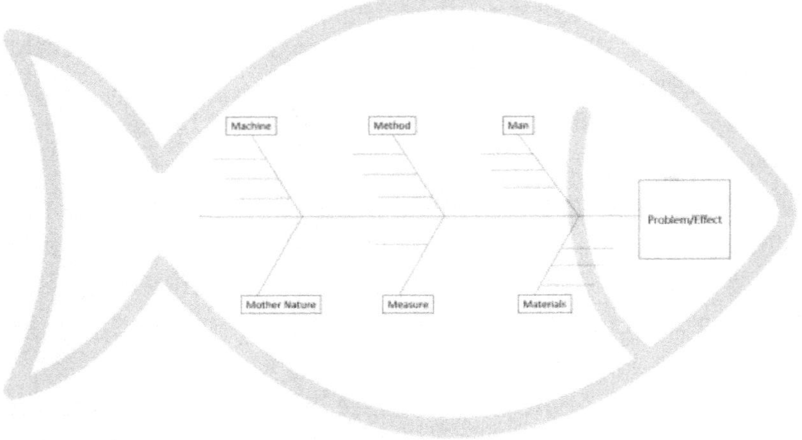

The head of the "fish" is the problem/topic (also called the effect). The "bones" of the fish are the predefined categories: Man, Method, Machine, Mother Nature, Measure, and Materials. As you brainstorm your ideas to solve your problem, sort those ideas into the listed categories. There is NO right or wrong here, as the categories are simply a guide to help spark your ideas. The most important aspect is to get all of the ideas on that diagram.

Your finished product can look like this:

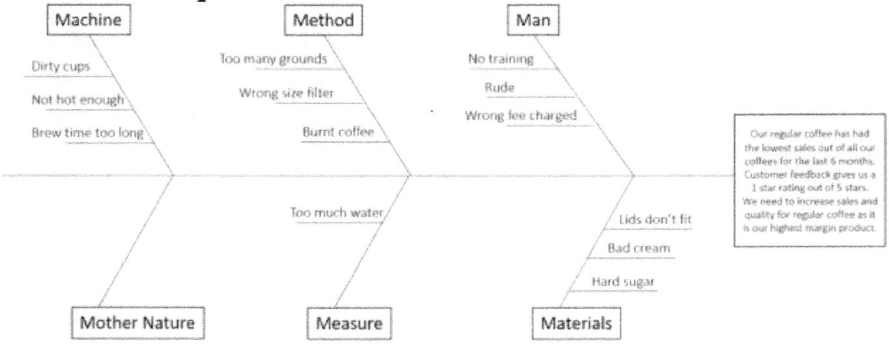

Once completed you can determine which area(s) you will focus on first. Circle those areas (honestly and literally, so you remember what you selected). Now, go learn things! Go to work gathering more information, try to fix the issue (PDCA), or rule out possibilities. Bring your team back together to share your findings. If any of those things didn't work or didn't turn out to be the root cause, then cross them off the fishbone and move on to the next set. You can even add more to your diagram based on what you learned. It's creativity and organization all in one!

I remember working with a team of people who were trying to solve a pretty important problem. The problem was listed as *hot, top priority*, and "*drop everything and work on it*" because the main person impacted was the head of the company. When I got involved the situation was a proverbial bowl of soup sprinkled with a dash of chaos and a smidge of anxiety.

They had SO MANY ideas for how to solve this problem, but they had a few obstacles:

1) They never kept track of what everyone was working on.
2) They didn't document the outcomes of their investigations.
3) They had no idea if their individual contributions made a positive (or negative) impact on someone else's task.

Yikes. I could just see all of these ingredients floating around in that proverbial soup, never cooking at the same time, and certainly never meshing together to create a delectable result.

I started drawing a fishbone diagram on the whiteboard. They all looked at me with a blank stare (maybe the same face you are making right now as you're reading this book). Most likely, they were thinking, "So what? How is that going to help us today?" Or, "Whatever, lady. We don't need some fancy tool to solve this."

It's true, they might not have needed a "fancy" tool like this to help solve their problem, but their current tools weren't working, so why not?

The problem was their inability to access company systems from any device. The problem statement looked similar to this:

The leader of our company (John) can only access company systems from any of his three devices (phone, laptop, and tablet) when he is plugged into the system using an ethernet cord (which means he is out of luck on his Wi-Fi/cellular phone). This has been happening over the last month. If he was on Wi-Fi, none of the systems could be accessed.

I wrote this statement on the "head" of the fish. As the team shared with me their ideas of how to fix this situation or what to investigate further, I documented each suggestion on the fishbone diagram, giving my best guess on which category to place each piece of information. There is NO right or wrong here. The categories are just a guide to help spark your ideas. The most important aspect is to get all of the ideas on that diagram.

After we completed the diagram, we reviewed and decided which of the ideas to focus on first. We held subsequent meetings to document the outcome of the investigation, crossing items off the drawing, until they FINALLY determined what was causing the problem and permanently fixed it!

As I already mentioned, those "standard" categories are just a guide. Feel free to change them to work best for your situation.

Is a relocation in your future? What are all of the things you need to consider when buying a new house? Location, cost, taxes, upkeep, size of property, number of bedrooms, number of bathrooms, basement, septic vs. city sewer, city water vs. well, landscaping, safety, privacy, insurance, garage size, outbuildings, neighborhood bi-laws/restrictions, sidewalks, playground, community pool, etc. This is not an exhaustive list, but still it is extensive.

This is what that list would look like as a fishbone diagram. Think of the possibilities! You could take this whenever you go to look at houses, and you could share it with your agent. It could serve as your checklist when walking through a house. This diagram outlines your requirements in a clear manner that is easy to understand.

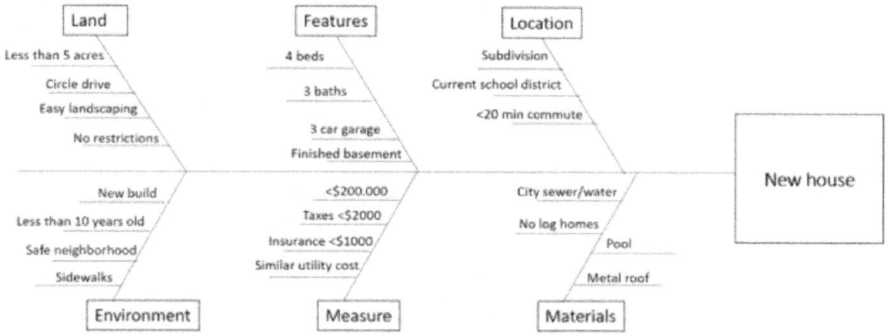

What would a fishbone diagram look like for a decision you are contemplating or a problem you are trying to solve? Maybe a fishbone could help you decide if you are going to keep your kids learning virtually next year, or if you'll send them back to school. Create a fishbone for that issue at work that is bugging you the most. This could be the "bait" you need to kickstart your ideas and solve your process problems!

CHAPTER THIRTEEN: MAP MY (PROCESS) RIDE

Value Stream Mapping

Earlier in the book we talked about the three versions of a process. Let's review:

1. The process that exists in a document. This could be the process description in your standard work, work instruction, visuals, or even on a recipe card.
2. The process as it "looks" in your head. This is what you think is happening when you visualize the process.
3. The way the process *actually* works. This is what really happens when you put action to the instructions.

Each of these versions of a process can be vastly different from the others. Let's look at a tool to understand what is REALLY going on with a process.

Have you ever used one of the apps on your phone that connects to your GPS and gives you an overhead visual of your ride, hike, walk, etc.? It's kind of neat to look at your journey from that perspective, and sometimes it doesn't look anything like what you thought it should be. In a similar way, we can map out our process (old school), using the concepts of value stream mapping.[16]

What's a value stream? A value stream is a series of actions to deliver value to the customer. For example, the process to create a quote for a customer is a value stream. The process to get to work each day is a value stream. The steps you take when you go for your doctor visit are a value stream. You get the point.

So how is value defined? Our customers defines value. Remember them? We realized who ALL of our customers are when we did a SIPOC.

There are three types of value: *value add, business non value add,* and *non value add.*

Value add is something that a customer would be willing to pay for (with real money or "funny" money, if they are internal customers). Value add changes the product (or in manufacturing we can say that "it changes form, fit, or function"), and value add is doing it right the first time. Doing it right the first time doesn't mean we are perfect (heck no!). It means we have a repeatable process with predictable results. Value add examples include: shipping the product, successfully making product changes based on customer requirements, and even the process of making their favorite lunch for your hungry kids.

Business non value add happens when we have to do something for the customer due to requirements or regulations, but it doesn't make our final product any better. If you do work for the government, you know there is certain paperwork you need to complete. It doesn't make your product any better, but if you don't complete it, you can't be a government contractor. (Some could say taxes are business non value add...but I digress.)

Non value added activities are those that utilize resources, but add no value. These are otherwise known as WASTE! Remember...DOWNTIME!

All of these are from the customer's perspective, so the value is personal and subjective. You may find value in a part of the process, but perhaps I don't. The doctor's office seems to find value in asking me for my insurance card every time I go for a visit, but I don't (at least not at the moment). You may find value in the wine of the month club, but your mother thinks you are crazy for spending your money on that subscription. (Hello, Mom. Live my life for a bit!)

In a value stream map, we physically map out the way our process actually works. We also indicate where there is waste and value add (or not) activities. At the end, we have a physical (or virtual) map depicting every single step in our process. There are several books that you can read on the "proper" way to create a value stream map.[17]

A value stream map represents the current reality, a realistic map of a process.

Go ahead, be curious, and Google it now. I'll wait.

Welcome back. Those look kind of scary, don't they? That's why I don't use the "textbook" value stream maps. People tend to get wrapped around the axel regarding the "proper" way to draw the map and what symbol to use. Listen, I am not the value stream police. No tickets issued here. I keep it simple.

A value stream map represents reality. The "Let's face it—it's this broken" reality. It's totally okay for your map to look like a mess, and it's totally okay if you discover your process has...can you guess...over 95% waste! We make these maps to reveal opportunity for improvement, so we start with what our baseline, or reality, looks like today.

Start with the process or value stream that you want to improve. Dare we say, the process that bugs you the most. Make sure it's reasonable, and the scope isn't too large. For example, we don't want to draw a value stream map for the process from receiving the customer order through shipment for a manufacturing company. We would be mapping for a LONG time. But we could map the purchasing or quoting process. I know someone who completed a value stream map for how they were currently loading their dishwasher. (Yes, really. No, not me.)

Let's go back to your scope. Where does the process in question begin and end? From the moment you load the dishes in the dishwasher until the cycle is complete, or when you put everything away?

Assemble your team. You need some people to help you with your map. At a minimum in attendance you need to have the person who works on the process, and the person responsible for that process and/or value stream. Most managers don't know how to do their employees' jobs, and that isn't where they should invest their time, so you want the folks that actually do the job, not their managers. It is also great to involve your customers and suppliers. (Epiphany moment: this is why you did that SIPOC earlier).

Dedicate time and space (physical or virtual) to get this done. Depending on the scope of what you are looking at, the process can take you anywhere from a few hours to a few days to complete. Try to get it done in one shot, or in continuous sessions. If you have too much time between your sessions, you will waste time playing catch up as you review where you were before.

Remember that you are essentially drawing the roadmap of your process, so we need some room to work. You need:

- Whiteboard or large piece of paper (think butcher paper)[4]
- Markers and pens
- Yellow sticky notes for ideas
- Another color sticky note to designate waste (I usually use a bright color like red or pink)

Remember two shapes: an oval and a diamond. If you took the little detour to Google-land a few paragraphs ago, then you know that there are pages listing the "correct" symbols to use in a value stream map. But if you follow along with me, there are only two that I need you to remember: **An oval for the start and the end markers, and a diamond shape for a decision.** That's it!

Begin with the word Start. Every value stream map begins with an oval with the word "Start" inside of it. Don't skip this step! You would be amazed how many I have seen that don't have a start!

Write down each step. On your individual yellow sticky notes write down each step in your process, including time required for that step. For example, if you are looking at a process that uses a specific system, the map would start to look like this:

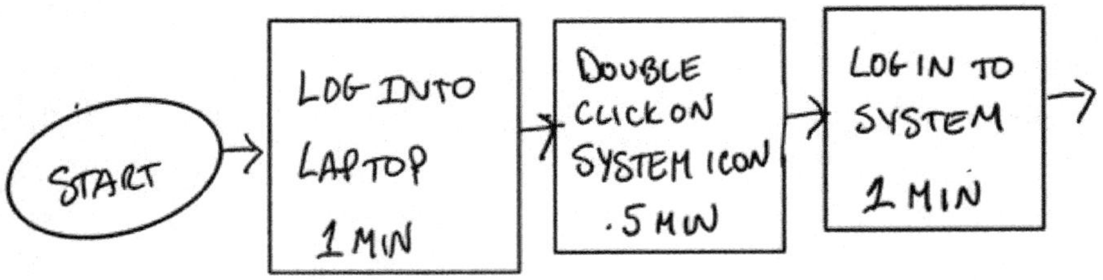

Stick with a standard, hours or minutes. Make sure you write down approximately how long it takes you to complete each task, as we will add all of those up at the end. If you start to mix the standard, you will get confused later when you go to add up the total time, so stick with hours and minutes. Keep working through each step of the process.

Identify any waste in each step. (Remember: DOWNTIME). If there is waste in that step, put the other colored sticky note behind that step. This is a GREAT visual to see just how much waste is in the process.

A strange thing happens when you are doing this. People either over simplify their process by combining steps (don't do that), or they get uncomfortable with seeing all the waste in the process so they give a general overview (don't do that either). Remember, we are not here to see how pretty your process is. This is not a reflection of someone "screwing up" or not following directions, so it's not a personal attack on anyone. We are working to investigate the process that is broken or not performing—NOT the person! It's not Scott's fault that the quoting process takes 12 days to complete. It is the process that he is following that is producing an undesirable outcome.

Reflect reality. The "current state" value stream, the way your process looks today, should depict reality as closely as possible. If you can't remember how that one part of the process works or what it looks like, then do two things:

1) **Call in an expert**. Some people call them the SME (subject matter expert), i.e., the Jimmy Hendrix (best guitarist ever) of your process. They know it inside and out.
2) **Go to where the work is being done**. Walk out on that manufacturing floor to see how the process actually works. Go to the desk of your internal customer in the finance department. Ask questions (nicely, not with *that* voice or tone). Learn things and then come back to your map and finish up. This is called going to the "Gemba." Physically (or virtually) observing where the work is being done.

Read aloud. Once you feel that your map is complete, take a break for a few minutes, and then read through it again—out loud. Because you are so laser focused on each step, one at a time, you may have missed something along the way. You may discover an output you forgot or a down line process that is impacted. Add anything that you may have forgotten and read through it again until it correctly represents your process.

Add up the time. The next step is to add up all the time from each process step and determine how much waste (%) there is in your process. Honestly, I usually see 95%-98% waste in a process when we do a map like this. The time, waste percentage, and map will now serve as your baseline for improvement.

Expect to be tired. This can be an emotional journey for some. At the end of the day, many people feel like they have "mashed potato" brains. You're done, spent, kaput and don't have anything else to give. Your brain is empty. And that's exactly how we like it. This is hard work, but SO worth it.

Here's an example of a value stream map for loading the dishwasher:

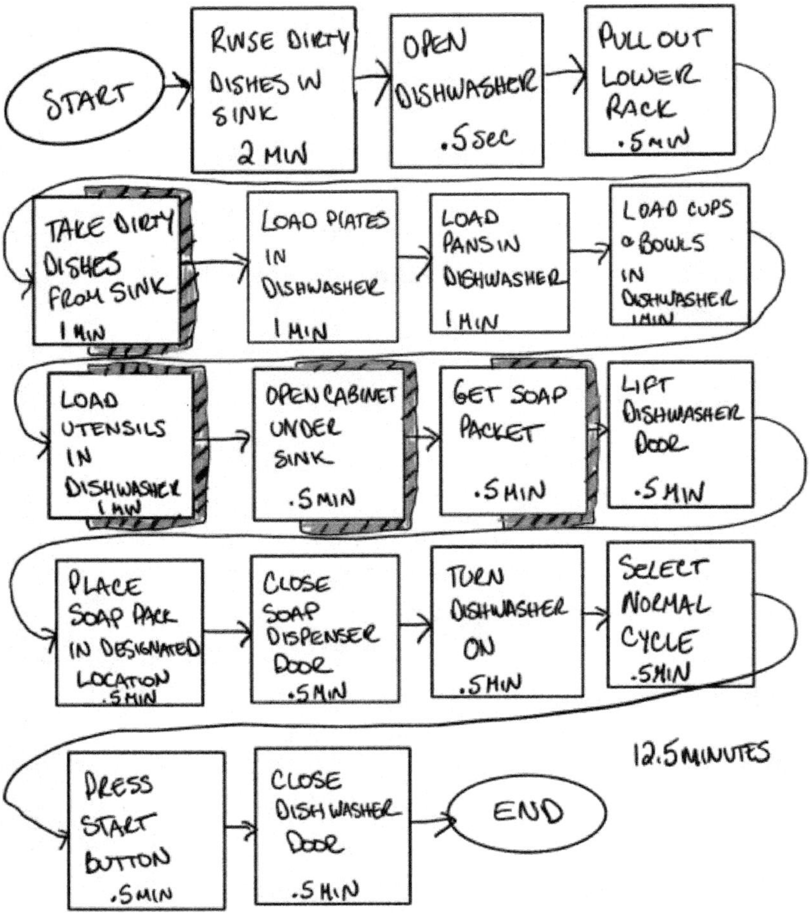

Now it's your turn. Pick a process: getting the kids ready for school, doing your homework, completing the PITA report at work, creating a contract for a new construction build, or writing up the legal document to create an LLC. Create a value stream map for your process, and come to terms with reality. Reality might not be pretty, but it's a great place to start. Now is the time when the magic begins. We come to terms with what things look like today, and we start to imagine what could be.

CHAPTER FOURTEEN: IMAGINE ALL THE PEOPLE-WITH GREAT PROCESSES!

Ideal State

When I was a little girl, I used to LOVE to draw. I could take any image and draw it myself. I especially loved to draw Disney characters and scenes. And then one day, it all stopped. Maybe someone said something to me that made me feel self conscious about my drawings, or I felt it was a "childish" way to spend my time when I should be studying (verified #1 nerd here). Faster than a toddler with something they shouldn't have in their mouth, *poof!* Gone.

Have you ever felt this way? Somewhere along the path of growing up, our sense of wonder and imagination gets buried beneath school, tests, clothing styles, friends, and the expectations of being an "adult." One minute you are daydreaming about life at Hogwarts, and it seems like the next minute you are an adult, paying bills, and worrying about insurance premiums. Where did all that creativity go?

Maybe you even labeled yourself as "not creative" along the way. Wow! What a limitation to put on yourself!

If you have ever thought of a "better" way to do something, *you are creative.*

If you have ever found a faster way to get to work (or, let's be honest, the fastest way to get home), *you are creative.*

If you have ever built a fort with blankets, *you are creative.*

If you figured out how to work a diaper genie, *you are creative.*

It's all there, and now it's time to let it shine!

Typically after we create a current state value stream map, we work on an "ideal state." (We do this in our *Kaizen* event which I'll talk about later.) Our ideal state is all that we can dream and hope for in an improved process.

Our ideal state is all that we can dream and hope for in an improved process.

But before we talk about ideals, I invite the group to "mentally leave the room" for a few minutes. I need to take their brains to another place, to break those established neural pathways for a bit. I am not talking about ice breakers here. I am talking about warming up parts of your brain you don't always use on a daily basis. I am talking about quick, fun games to help people relax and escape. I often use brain teasers like:

A man pushes his car to a hotel and tells
the owner he's bankrupt. Why?
He's playing Monopoly!

Forrest left home running. He ran a ways and then
turned left, ran the same distance and turned left again,
ran the same distance and turned left again. When he got
home, there were two masked men. Who were they?
The catcher and the umpire!

A cowboy gallops into town on Monday, stays for two
days and leaves town on Monday. How can that be?
His horse's name is Monday!

I also use games like "Salute the King" or "The Great Candy Pass."[5]

Stop rolling your eyes. Don't knock it until you have tried it! It works, and it breaks up your thinking process, even for a few minutes. After your brain is loose enough to do the camel pose in yoga, we start our ideal state activity.

What if you could ask for ANYTHING you wanted to fix a situation? That is what ideal state is all about. No limits. Pie in the sky. Wave your magic wand. Click your ruby slippers together. Anything you want. Tell me what it is.

Now start coming up with ideas for the ideal state of that thing that's bugging you, whether it's a wasteful process or the dream of where you'd like to retire. Start thinking. Don't criticize anyone's ideas, and especially do not criticize yours before they come out of your mouth. Turn that filter off for a bit.

On a big piece of paper (like one of those 3' tall sticky notes), **write down ALL of the ideas for the topic at hand** (process improvement, retirement location, budget ideas, etc.). You could even open your tablet and start writing on a blank note page. Write them all down.

Maybe you'd like an "easy button," with the ability to press one button to automatically generate a report so you don't have to do anything else, or your ideal state could be one button shipping of your product instead of filling out forms and labels. How about different colors on the screens in the system to make it easier to remember what screen you are working on since they all look the same today? Perhaps a warning screen that pops up to show potential errors before you exit the screen? Maybe you'd like notification when you have reached a certain level on your credit card. Are you considering a retirement location that has golf courses nearby and you are allowed to drive your cart on the road? Dreaming of a destination that has 300+ days of sunshine each year? (Arizona, here we come!)

WRITE IT ALL DOWN.
NO FILTERS.
NO MENTAL CRITICISM!

Keep going. Keep writing until there is nothing left, and then write down more ideas. Your (virtual or physical) page should be covered with ideas. It doesn't have to be pretty, and spelling never counts.

Give yourself at least 30 minutes (or more) to do a brain dump of all of the things you wish it could be. What would make your life easier? What do you want? What do you need? Don't limit your ideas based on your current state. Let it all go from your head, your heart, and to your fingers to document.

Once you are *done-done*, take a step back and **review your idea page**. Read your ideas aloud, and ask for any clarification needed. Remember, you still don't get to criticize or critique these ideas. Put down your red pen! You should be astonished and proud of all the extraordinary ideas you (and possibly your team) have listed.

Now what? What do we do with all of these phenomenal ideas?

Believe it or not, on average at least 80% of those ideas become reality in our future. Yes, really, so this time has not been wasted. These possibilities will serve as the foundation for the future, and we call that *future state*. Whether it's the way we improve our process or our final decision on a retirement location, these things matter. The solutions were probably locked deep inside your brain, and you may not have known they were there. They needed an ideal space to come out of hiding.

CHAPTER FIFTEEN: THE FUTURE'S SO BRIGHT

Future State

Now that you have come up with the impressive list to fix your report or streamline your dishwasher loading/unloading process, it's time to make that a reality!

A future state documents how we want things to work in the future. Remember that you need to really understand your current situation or process before you can improve it, but this is NOT a copy/paste from the current state value stream map you have completed. A future state value stream map is not all about eliminating steps, it's about working more efficiently and eliminating waste from your (now documented) current state value stream map.

How can you peek into the future to understand what the process will look like?

1. Review and recognize the opportunities for improvement or desires for a better future in your current state. If you have not completed a current state value stream map, then simply document your current state. This may look like, "I am going to retire from the U.S. Post Office in five years," or "I just found out I am pregnant with twin girls, and I need to figure everything out before they are born on February 28."

2. Review your ideal state list.
3. Start mapping or writing out what you want the future to look like.

4. Try it out, and see if it is going to work for you! (remember PDCA!)

Similar guidelines to your value stream map apply here:

You need help! To craft your future, assemble the same people who helped you with your current state value stream (map or list). **You need dedicated time and space** (physical or virtual) to complete this tool. Really, try to get it done in one shot, hopefully all in one day (2-4 hours), or in continuous sessions. If you have too much time between your sessions, you will lose momentum and magic.

You need:

- White board or large piece of paper (think butcher paper)
- Markers and pens
- Yellow sticky notes for ideas
- Other colored sticky notes to designate waste. [6]

Remember that you are essentially putting your vision/dreams into a physical representation of reality, so we need some room to work.

◆ ◆ ◆

When I work with a group on a current state map they constantly throw out ideas for what we "should" do in the future. I write those down in a spot called the "Parking Lot," so we can revisit them later.

Guess what happens when we start to document the future state? They clam right up. Their mouths and their brains are suddenly zipped up tight. I always think, "Wait! What just happened here?"

There's a nasty little four-letter word to describe this scenario: FEAR. Fear of the unknown. Fear of looking or sounding "dumb." Fear that it won't work. Fear that someone is going to get blamed for something.

What would happen if we thought of FEAR in a different way:

Fabulously Evolving And Reinventing

Would you be willing to try something new if you defined fear that way?

◆ ◆ ◆

Begin by making your oval with the word "Start" inside of it. Now, using your sticky notes, write down the individual steps in your NEW process. You might not have the actual "times to complete" available, as this is all new, but give it your best estimate.

As you work compare the map of your new process to the map of your current state, and make sure: 1) you are not copy/pasting all of those exact steps into your future state, and 2) you are eliminating the opportunities for waste.

Identify areas where you can create a "work around" to make a task easier to complete (also called Poka Yoke[18] in Japanese). Look into mistake proofing to keep people from putting a square peg in a round hole. How can you set up a process that prevents anyone from making a mistake?

Refer back to your ideal state. Don't let those ideas go to waste. Put them in there! Recall that an average of 80% of the items in your idea state actually become reality in your future state. Where could you implement these impressive ideas into your new process?

When you are done with your future state, it doesn't end with "And let it be so." Conclude with a list of actions, owners, and follow up commitments. If your future state assumes that part of your report will be automated, then someone has to commit to follow up with IT to understand the possibilities and timelines. Another someone (probably you) must begin researching the best child safe cribs on the planet that will fit into that designated location in the guest room which is now your twins' nursery. And your real estate agent will start looking for your ideal retirement community based on the specifications.

Follow up on these actions within 30 days at the most. If you wait any longer they will get lost and forgotten in the shuffle of other decisions. If the actions aren't completed, then schedule a follow up session within another 30 days (or less). Update your future state document with the results of any action items. Most importantly, maintain the forward momentum and enthusiasm from this activity. Good things are coming your way.

Look at the difference in these two maps.

Current state:

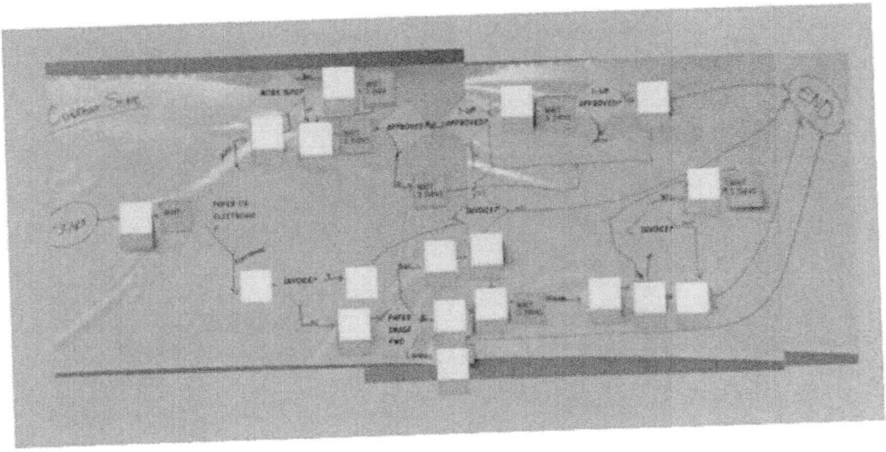

Same process, future state. Impressive, right?

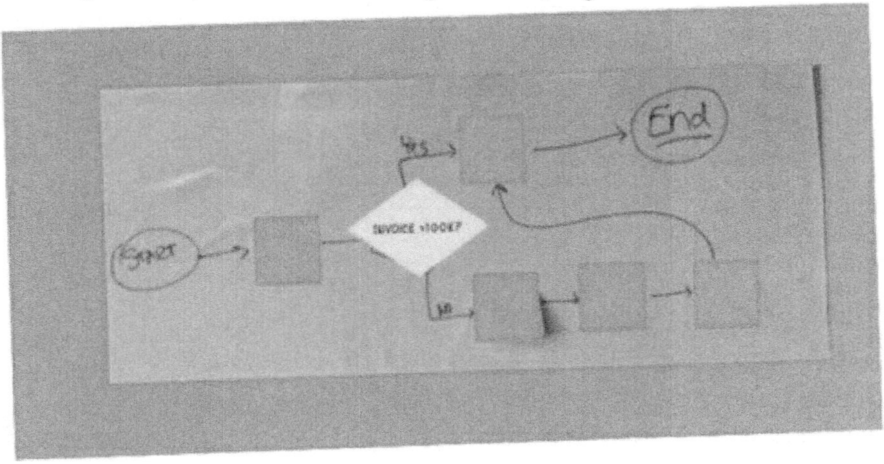

Here are the maps for our dishwasher dilemma. In the current state it was taking 12.5 minutes to load the dishwasher. The spoons and forks came out dirty 80% of the time, and based on how the items were originally loaded, there was wasted motion when emptying the dishwasher.

On the current state value stream map we noted a few areas in red/stripes where we think we can make improvements: taking the dirty dishes from the sink, loading the utensils, opening the cabinet, and getting the soap packet.

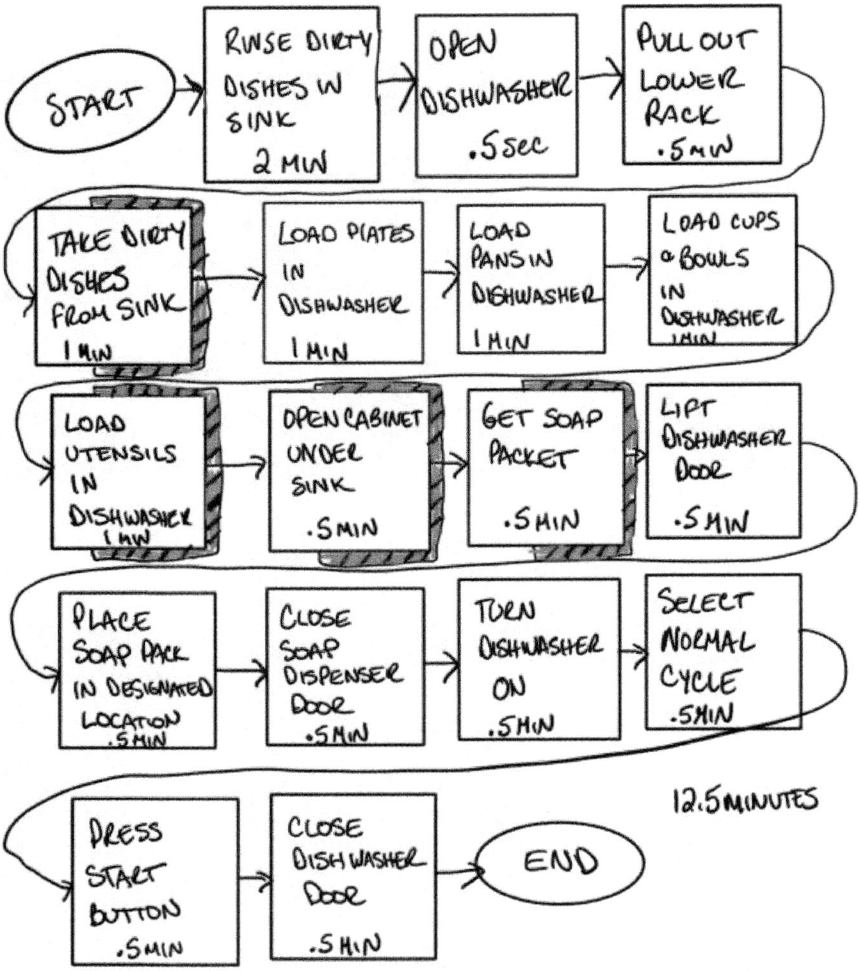

Here is the future state process map for loading the dishwasher. You may notice there are (green) stars by the processes that have changed. This is a great visual for everyone to recognize an update to the dishwasher process.

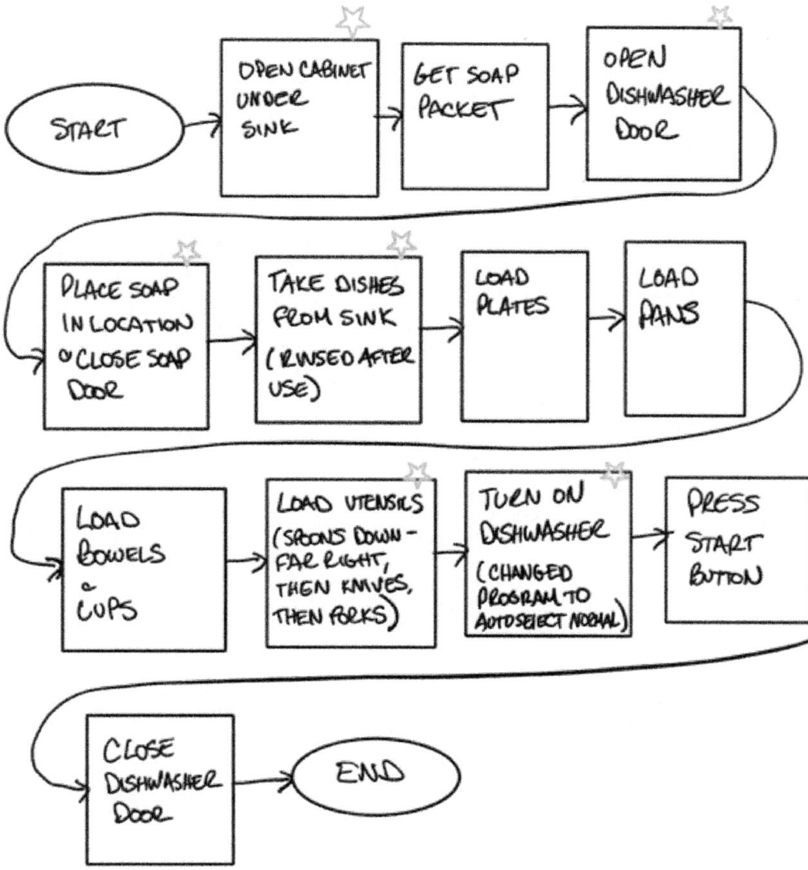

As you can see, we put the soap right away in the dishwasher. We also began rinsing our plates before we put them in the sink (you could make another improvement by rinsing and putting the plates in the dishwasher right after eating). We used a new method to load utensils in order to fix the problem with them not coming out clean, and to make it more efficient when unloading the dishwasher. We also reprogrammed the dishwasher so that the default wash setting is "normal."

Once you have implemented your future state (or modified future state), review the outcome in 30, 60, 90, or even 120 days. This will allow time for any necessary behavior modifications, updates to documentation, and to realize the savings you have recovered. Every minute saved allows you to do more value added work that can impact your bottom line, especially if you operate a small business where every penny counts. What a rare opportunity we have with this tool, as we don't always get to control the destiny of a process or situation. Here we can make it as efficient as you want/need it to be.

Imagine the possibilities, and map out your future state for any process you choose: getting the kids ready for school, doing your homework, completing that PITA report at work, creating a contract for a new construction build, or writing up the legal document to create an LLC. Create actions to make this a reality! Remember: you are organized, and you are creative. You got this!

CHAPTER SIXTEEN: HERD THE CATS OR TAKE THEM ONE AT A TIME

Batch vs. One Piece Flow

My husband often tells me that instead of making a dozen chocolate chip cookies, I should just make one giant one like they do at the mall for your birthday. First off, do I look like Mrs. Fields? No, not even close. Secondly, don't you think the rest of the family would enjoy some cookies, and not a piece broken off the giant one you just bit into? Yes, yes, we would like some cookies without your germs, please and thank you. There are benefits to making a whole batch instead of just one.

Have you gone through an insurance open enrollment process lately? Those poor people in your HR department or with the government, they get hit all at once with a million different questions. They also have to make sure everything is in order when they send over the information to the insurance providers on December 15. There are literally dire consequences for screwing up that process! Talk about stress!

But, let's consider the alternative. What would this look like if they didn't do an annual enrollment process for everyone all at one time? Maybe they could decide to switch to a process based on your hire date every year. Do you think that would make things easier or harder for you and your company (or agency)? I used to work for a company that has over 120,000 employees around the world. Enrolling one person at a time for their insurance sounds much better conceptually, but managing that long term process, especially with that many people, would be a nightmare. And, it would limit the "buying" power of the company if everyone began their insurance (and premiums) on different dates.

The cookies and the annual enrollment processes are examples of two different concepts: batch and one piece flow. We can use these concepts to help make improvements to our situations at work and at home. Let's look at a few more examples:

Paying all the bills for each week on Friday: batch
Paying the bills as they come in during the week: one piece flow

Creating an "assembly line" to make school lunches all at the same time: batch
Creating individual lunches one at a time: one piece flow

Going to Starbucks and ordering a venti soy caramel macchiato: one piece flow
Going to Subway and ordering a turkey sandwich, plain: one piece flow

Buying all of your holiday presents from Amazon: batch
Buying three bags of softener salt at the hardware store: batch

Let's start by looking at the pros and cons of each.

The concept behind batch is to "build up" orders to a certain level in order to reduce average cost. What does that mean?

It means you lay out eight slices of bread, smooth peanut butter on four of them, add a layer of jelly on each one, and finally place the remaining four naked pieces of bread on top. You have four PB&J sandwiches for your family, instead of making one at a time for four people.

Instead of making one cell phone at a time, you carry a tray of 10 models as a batch, completing each individual process for all 10 at once.

Sounds logical, doesn't it? It is... to some extent. However, there are occasions when batching doesn't make sense, and actually makes things worse.

In a manufacturing setting, by batching the production, you can create excess inventory between steps. When there is a quality defect found it can be more challenging to determine where it came from with a batch process. You are also more likely to have to scrap (throw out) the entire batch when an issue is found. There goes that entire tray of iPhone XYZ's.

One piece flow is all about making one item at a time to precisely meet customer demand. I like to use the phrase "make one, move one" or MOMO.

When I go to Starbucks, the baristas make one cup of my fancy beverage just the way I like it. They don't have a big vat of Vanilla Latte sitting around. No, they make it per my specifications, just one cup.

One piece flow is onboarding new employees as they join the company, only on the 15th and 30th of the month, instead of onboarding them in a group.

It is also sending one cell phone at a time all the way through the production process instead of a tray of them (batch). When an issue is found in station 10 out of 20, they can pinpoint the root cause faster and fix it. (Or, just scrap one phone, instead of a tray of 10.)

Is one concept better than the other? No! It depends on the situation and your desired outcome.

I remember working with a client who always sent all their bank information from the entire week to the bank on Friday at 3 PM. Guess what happened on Friday at 4 PM? Phones started ringing and inboxes started to fill up. There were issues with the feed...again. The accounting team routinely had to work until late every single Friday to resolve the issues (which doesn't make for happy team members). There was no time to waste, as those entries needed to be posted no later than Friday at midnight. That's an example of a traditional batch process.

How did they fix it? They first spoke about implementing one piece flow. On paper that sounded like a great plan. However, once they checked with their customer (back to your SIPOC concept: their customer is the bank), one piece flow wasn't optimal for the banking systems. They ended up changing their process to send the bank information every day at 5 PM. This allowed them to quickly identify any issues the next morning, and they could work to fix them before the next run at 5 PM the following day. The impact of this change was immediate. Long standing issues that were usually addressed with a band-aid on a weekly basis were now brought to light and resolved. (Honestly, they got tired of seeing that same error every single day.) The bank was happier with the reduced number of issues, and everyone was able to go home at a decent hour on Friday. Win-win-win.

One piece flow also allows us to receive "real time" data which is a hot topic everywhere. Do you want to have to wait for the shift to complete on the production line to see how much you have in WIP (work in process)? Or do you want to know where your customer products are each step of the way? Real time data.

Do you want to sit at the airport terminal, wondering if your flight is leaving on time, or do you want to be able to get a text message if that time changes? Real time data.

Do you want to know if you passed a really hard online exam as soon as you are done? Real time data.

Is batch better than one piece at a time? It depends on your desired outcomes.

This information isn't intended to knock batch processing. Sometimes batch just makes sense like in our annual enrollment process. It makes more sense to batch this activity to complete every November rather than on your hire date. It's more efficient to batch your annual performance review process for every October rather than on your hire date. A batch process organizes and combines all of those activities that surround it into a timeline for everyone to complete. Training is done all at the same time, and all employees work on self-appraisals at the same time. It also allows companies to forecast more accurately based on a consolidated annual review process.

In our barn we measure out the grain for our horses once a month, and we store their meals in labeled plastic containers. This saves the time of having to scoop and measure for all three of them twice a day. If you are making four PB&J sandwiches, it just makes sense to make them in a batch rather than one at a time.

Where are you currently batching and seeing issues emerge? Are you batching your laundry, and finding pink underwear that used to be white? The answer is not to abandon batches and implement one piece flow, or it would take a REALLY long time to wash clothes for a house with four people! Maybe you need to change the way that you batch your laundry loads. Colors, towels, whites, and delicates, instead of just a batch of colors and whites.

How about an area that could use the one piece flow technique? You might be a counselor, consultant, or therapist and you need to submit claims to your client's insurance company for your services. Switch to one piece flow by giving yourself time between clients to complete this paperwork instead of trying to complete it all at the end of the day when you are tired and spent (any kind of paperwork—real or electronic—isn't fun.)

When you are cooking take out the ingredients that you need as you need them, and then put them back where they belong right away. That's one piece flow, instead of waiting until after you serve your meal, and then you have a major disaster to clean up in the kitchen.

When you set out your outfit the night before, instead of staring blankly into your closet in the morning while running late for work, you are utilizing one piece flow.

Cookies or coffee, reports or sandwiches, figure out what works best for you with the least amount of waste: DOWNTIME.

CHAPTER SEVENTEEN: DOING IT THE SAME WAY EVERY TIME

Standard Work

Why do you follow grandma's handwritten recipe on a 3x5 card to make her cheesecake? Why do pilots go through a pre-flight checklist prior to taking off? Why does your doctor take your blood pressure every time you go see her? It's all standard work!

Standard work is the most powerful lean tool in the world! (You have to say that in your head with the voice of the announcer from WWF.) We use standard work so that we can have the same result each time, whether that is a fantastic cheesecake (that really tastes like grandma's) or a safe flight, standard work allows for consistency. If we follow it, we should have the same result time after time.

We use standard work so we can have the same result, time after time.

Standard work is known by a few other names: work instruction, standard operating procedure (SOP), job aids, etc. It documents how we currently perform the work. The key word here is "currently," and these processes have to be up-to- date for a reason: to ensure everyone is doing it the exact same way. With a standard, repeatable process we will see predictable results (also known as reduced variation). And, of course, I've shown you what happens when I don't follow that standard work: I get to work without my car keys!

We use standard work to train team members as this documents how they do their job or specific task. It also provides the baseline for improvement. We use our standard work documents when we are beginning our journey to process improvement. Standard operating procedures (SOPs) are our baseline. We use it during our current state value stream map. We update our standard work based on the final outcome of our future state value stream map. Standard work reflects the way things need to be done, every time, until we improve it.

Keep in mind that your standard work documents should be easy to understand by the person/people that are doing the work. The standard work for the manufacturing lines of one of the largest automobile makers in the world is all images. What?! Sounds crazy, doesn't it? Their thought pattern is twofold: 1) their process should be easy enough to explain with images, and 2) there is no need for language translations!

Our standard work documents support audits (again, because we are assuming that the standard work documentation reflects the way you *really* complete that process/task). Instead of showing someone how you put that journal entry into the system, you can provide them with the documented steps of how exactly that happens, every time, by any person.

Your standard work should be stored in an area that is easily accessible. I don't want to be searching through endless drawers in my kitchen to find grandma's recipe card, so I place all of her recipe cards in a recipe box (and/or scan them into my tablet for quick reference). All of the standard work at a company could be stored on a SharePoint site or electronic document management system. This also ties back to the concept of 5S, ensuring that ALL of your standard work is in one place, always. That one place will always contain the most up-to-date versions.

I once worked with a team to establish a new process to onboard middle school students and/or transfer students newly enrolled in a local high school. When we mapped out that process and asked about the standard work, the team had to take a quick break to check into their system to access the most "up-to-date" documentation.

Guess what we found? *There were over 98 documented SOPs for how to onboard a new student to high school! 98!* That's crazy! How did that happen? The right hand didn't talk to the left hand. As people improved/changed the process, they created new documents instead of updating the old. People retired and new people came in. When they couldn't find the standard work for onboarding, they made a version of their own. No one ever searched their system to see what currently existed for this process. I am happy to say that there is now one, yes, one, standard work document for this process!

Standard work can energize your team. I bet you think I am kidding, right? Remember, everyone is unique, and some people find comfort in having a document to reference so they can be certain that they are doing their job or a process correctly. They love black and white instructions with no room for interpretation. They get excited knowing they are "doing the right thing."

Sometimes when we are looking at process improvement opportunities, the best place to start is to look at the current standard work. It is one indicator of how things are working now, or supposed to work, so we can continue to make necessary improvements.

Standard work is also an opportunity for a team to collaborate. Even if you are working with a team of two, the process should be completed collectively. Creating standard work can seem like a mundane task, but it allows us to become intentional about our actions. We can be continuous learners about our own process and the processes of others.

Key reminders about standard work:

- Make sure they exist (with preferably only one version of the "truth")
- Know where to find them

- Ensure they reflect reality
- Update them as you make improvements

If you have a sinking feeling right now that you don't have any standard work, or maybe you don't know where to find it, then good: I have done my job. Create the standard work that doesn't exist! It doesn't have to be fancy. A simple document with numbered steps is a great start. If you don't know the standard work at your company, ask! You can standardize anything—I even have standard work for my weekly trip to the grocery store. I create my list the same way every time so I don't forget anything.

Veggies	Dairy	Meat
Clean	Miscellaneous	

Look before you leap into something new! Take that cheesecake recipe on your 3x5 card in your old, brown recipe box on the top shelf above the stove, and update it for future generations. Someday they'll be thankful it tastes just like yours, every time.

CHAPTER EIGHTEEN: BRINGING IT ALL TOGETHER

Kaizen

Throughout this book, you may have noticed few words that might not be in your "normal" vocabulary. Poka Yoke, Ishikawa, Gemba, and now Kaizen. These are Japanese terms that we regularly use in the world of continuous improvement, lean and six sigma.[19] The original concept of Lean originated with Henry Ford in his Model T factory. As we all know, he was credited with creating the first moving assembly line.[20] Kiichiro Toyoda and Taiichi Ohno came from Japan to observe these concepts, and then they went back to perfect them even more. This is the reason we see a sprinkle of Japanese terms when we talk about Lean and continuous improvement.

Kaizen means "good change" in Japanese.

In a *kaizen* event, we bring a cross functional group of people together to solve a problem. Some people refer to these as a "continuous improvement event." We bring together the collective brain power of a group of people to solve a problem in rapid fashion. Many times there is over 100 years of combined experience with the attendees! This is where the magic happens.

We start by understanding the current situation and creating a measurable problem statement and corresponding goal. We first discussed problem statements with the concept of PDCA.

Without this we have no idea what problem we are trying to solve, who should be invited, what metrics are impacted, scope, etc. Our *kaizen* event would essentially consist of a room full of people sitting on their hands wondering why they were there.

Once we have established the problem, then we determine who is going to sponsor the event, how long it will take to complete, and who should participate. The sponsor is the person(s) ultimately responsible for the process (at a high level), and quite honestly, these are ones who will approve the time for everyone to step away from their "normal" jobs to do this. (Oh, and pay for lunch, too!)

I try not to scope out an event that will take longer than a week to complete, because many people just can't be away from their regular jobs for that long. Also, if we work too long on one problem, we encounter the Law of Diminishing Returns. My "normal" *kaizen* event takes 1-4 days depending on the size of the problem, scope, etc.

I have "rules" for the event. Not everyone likes them, but these are the rules for my events:

- We need you present, both mentally and physically.
- Laptop, cell phone, and tablet usage are permitted only during designated breaks (unless we are looking up information).
- Commit to stay with the team for the entire *kaizen* event (no leaving for other meetings or appointments).
- Respect each other.
- Teamwork is key.
- No idea is a bad idea.
- Focus on the process, NOT the person.
- Pay attention to the person speaking (no side conversations).
- Avoid analysis paralysis.
- Don't sit and spin!

Yes, everyone is present for the ENTIRE event. We do take frequent breaks, and I allow at least an hour for lunch.

Our typical agenda includes almost everything we have already covered in this book all wrapped up with one big bow: SIPOC, current state value stream map, ideal state, future state value stream map, action items, and reflection. We utilize the concepts of 5S, waste, PDCA, mistake proofing, visual management, kanban, batch, one piece flow, and standard work to improve the process under investigation.

A crazy thing happens when you bring people together for an event. If you watch closely, they go through the stages of team dynamics: forming, storming, norming, and performing,[21] right in front of your eyes. *Forming* is when we first come together. Everyone is nicey-nicey, all smiling and polite. *Storming* is the next stage when people start to test boundaries, speak up, and challenge each other. *Norming* is when we start to settle down, eventually finding our favorite spot to sit in that conference room or "your" parking spot in the parking deck. Finally, we get to *performing,* where we all start to work together and function like a decently well-oiled machine. I have seen teams go through this process in under 20 minutes, and I have also seen teams struggling to perform together even after eight hours. It's a journey, so don't expect everyone to click and start working in a symbiotic group right away.

Hansei is a Japanese term that means "self-reflection." This is typically done at the end of each day and/or at the conclusion of the event. *Hansei* is a time to reflect back on what was accomplished, what you learned, what shocked you, and what this all means to you. Just like most of the other tools, you can put people on the spot and do this verbally, or you can have people write down their ideas on sticky notes and put them on the wall. (I reference this as the "What stuck with you?" activity to be read aloud by the facilitator. See our Facebook page)[7] You routinely hear things like:

- "I had no idea there was that much waste in this pro-

cess."
- "I didn't know my process impacted you like that."
- "I learned how to use the SIPOC tool."
- "Now I know where our standard work is documented in the office."

The *Hansei* reflection is a great way to wrap up and conclude an event. Additionally, it offers a time to document decisions, assign action items, and schedule follow up meetings.

A *kaizen* event presents us with an opportunity to identify, analyze, and respond to risk. What is risk? Risk is anything that could go wrong when all the stars align and something bad happens as a result. For example, if you were a banking institution and you issued ATM cards with a brand new technology, what could possibly go wrong? You would list all of the things that could go wrong (within reason), and include how you are going to fix them when the situation arrives. If someone doesn't enter the pin correctly for the card three times, what are you going to do? Keep letting them try or lock their card?

Risk is also why you hear those disclaimers on the commercials for medicines (with side effects that sound worse than your original problem). In their studies they have shown that a certain percentage of people exhibited this reaction, so they need to disclose it as a risk. Remember the Ford Pinto case? This case offers a prime example of risks that were known, and NOTHING was done to prevent catastrophic situations.

Look for risk when you are analyzing the way things work today and will work in the future. Document it. Create a response to that risk, fix the situation, or lessen the impact. Every time you update that process (hello, it's continuous improvement!), you need to review and update the risks.

You can use a *kaizen* event in a variety of ways. I have used it for manufacturing, IT, Finance, HR, Legal, Travel, Quality, and small business issues. You can also use it for non-work related issues like solving a problem that exists within a non-profit, resolving a situation with a traveling athletic team, or fixing a situation within the PTA. All you need is a problem to solve and people to help you solve that problem in a rapid fashion.

Think of the way that you currently solve problems. Brainstorm the ways that a *kaizen* event may help you to stop playing paintball, and solve your problem in one shot!

CHAPTER NINETEEN: BUT DID YOU ASK?

Communication Problems

I remember working with a group of people who were very upset when they came to me. They wanted/needed a *kaizen* event right away. You could almost see the red emergency beacon lighting up on their heads. Keep in mind, especially in emotionally charged situations like this, 80% of what is coming out of their mouths are emotions, and only 20% is really the problem they are trying to solve—but they may not know it yet.

I said, "Tell me, what's the problem."

"We need a *kaizen* on this before the end of the month. We have a report that we need to automate ASAP."

"Okay, why does it need to be automated?"

"Because it is currently a manual process, and it takes Wanda all month to complete."

"Okay, manual isn't good, but tell me more."

"We have no idea how she does this report, no standard work or documentation."

Hmmm. I guess Wanda never went on vacation. Fantastic!

"Where does the report go? Who receives the report?"

"It gets emailed to an email box."

"A personal email box?" I asked.

"No, it goes to a group email box."

"Great! Who has access to that email box?"

They looked at one another. Nobody had a clue how to access

that email box. No clue.

"What do you do with the data?"

They collectively agreed, "We have no idea."

"Wow. Okay. And how long has this process been happening?"

"For over five years."

"And is there anything else I need to know?"

They looked at me sheepishly, and I knew I found the source of emotion: "Wanda is going to retire at the end of the month."

"And it's currently the 15th of the month," I said. "Alrighty then. This just keeps getting better and better."

We talked for a little while longer, starting to create the structure of a problem statement with the information we had. I suggested scheduling a meeting with people whom we think "might" be impacted by this process first before we move on to a full out *kaizen* event. They agreed, and we scheduled the meeting for the end of the week.

In my head I sounded like a Las Vegas preacher as I kicked off the meeting: "Ladies and gentleman, we are gathered here today because Wanda is retiring, and there appears to possibly be some opportunities in the report she manually completes each month. It currently takes her 40 hours to complete this report, and it is then emailed to the ABC email group. Does anyone in here access that email box and know what happens with the data?"

Before I could proceed any further, a gentleman waved his hand and stopped me.

"Excuse me, excuse me. Is this about Wanda's report? We automated that report two years ago, but we could never find anyone to own that process."

Mic drop. WHAT?

Yes, that team had completed an event to automate the manual reports they were receiving, and they had fully automated Wanda's report. But because that team didn't involve Wanda (or her boss) in that event, and because they didn't create any standard work, they had no idea it even happened. All they had to do was ask.

Do you really have a problem to solve (perhaps
with a full-blown *kaizen* event),
or do you have a simple lack of communication?

Communication can be our greatest savior or our worst enemy, both at work and at home. Regardless of the environment, ensure that you are communicating process changes, especially if you are a direct or indirect customer of that process. Before a *kaizen* event takes place bring all of the invitees together for a quick meeting to review the situation, and directly ASK if we forgot to invite someone. Refer back to your SIPOC to see who is impacted (or who impacts you). For example, tell your partner that you are now storing the cat's food in the freezer instead of the pantry to eliminate morning feeding chaos.

A great way to keep your communication channels organized is by creating a communication plan for your activity. List out who needs to receive communication, what type of communication they need to receive, and most importantly, HOW they would like to receive that communication. Some people dislike meetings that only provide an update on the status of a project (especially if everything is "green," meaning there are no issues). Other people want that meeting along with a presentation and an update to the internal documentation system. Know your audience. Understand what they want/need, and act accordingly. Don't assume because you might just be the one walking around with the red emergency beacon light on your head.

CHAPTER TWENTY: THIS IS NOT THE END

The Beginning of Your Journey

Wow! I can't believe we are done chatting already! I hope that you have learned a few things along the way, and I hope you learned that you now have the tools to improve your life at work and at home. When you started reading this book, you may have been thinking, "No way, I am NOT organized," but you went into your kitchen, looked at your utensil drawer organizer, and proved yourself wrong. I want you to remember that.

I also want you to remember that continuous improvement is a circle with no end, and we keep at it every single day because there are endless opportunities to improve (95% waste!). I want you to remember that if you have absolutely no idea where to start, look at what bugs you the most and begin there. Know within yourself that you can try to fix something, not quite fix it completely, start all over again (PDCA), and that's okay.

I want you to remember that we are aiming for the minimal viable product, not 100% perfect every time. I hope that you look around you and see a world of processes and possibilities, areas where you can make things better, more efficient, safer, in order to save time and money.

You can now understand how intertwined everything is. When we make changes, we have to remember who else we may impact (SIPOC). Don't forget that everyone has a kryptonite and a golden lasso (SWOT). I hope you'll remember that you have so many great ideas in your head, you just need to take the time to get them out on "paper" so you can start to do something about them (mind map, affinity diagram, fishbone).

I want you to never underestimate the power of making things visual: your processes, your instructions, your reminders (visual management, value stream mapping). Hopefully your child-like curiosity has returned (or at least you found it again), and I hope you realize that dreams can become a reality (ideal state, future state).

I hope you understand that there is a time and a place for coffees and cookies (batch and one piece flow). I hope you'll remember that the most powerful lean tool in the world is standard work, and how important it is to follow it (so you don't get to work without your car keys). I hope you'll remember that you can come together as a team to move mountains (*kaizen*), and communicating your success and challenges only makes you stronger.

I didn't come into my career thinking I was going to do this for the rest of my life. When I was a kid my future plans were a toss-up between becoming a teacher or a lawyer, or joining a band with my uncles. Truth! I ended up taking what I call the "alternatively long college approach." Let's just say it took me a while to complete my degree in management information systems, a combo of IT and Business. I always had some sense of organization with a little bit of OCD thrown in there for good measure.

It wasn't until I started working for a larger company that someone saw something in me that I didn't see myself. They tapped me on the shoulder and asked if I was interested in this kind of training, and I emphatically said, "NO!" Can you imagine? I initially said no to this opportunity that changed the trajectory of my entire career (and life). I said no because I didn't believe in myself, I didn't believe I could do all of these things, and I never imagined I could use all of these tools to really make a difference in my personal and professional life. That person saw something in me that I didn't see in myself at the time.

I see something in you, too. I see it in the organization of your utensil drawer.

You can improve absolutely anything.

Appendix

PRACTICAL TIPS AND TRICKS FOR CONTINUOUS IMPROVEMENT

How to Improve Absolutely Anything – Today

Car Keys

Does it drive you nuts to constantly lose your keys (or maybe your partner or kid loses them for you)? Simple solution: **Use a carabiner!**

Put your keys on the carabiner, and get into the habit of clipping it to your purse, backpack, bag, etc. You'll never lose your keys again if you use that carabiner and follow that process on a consistent basis. There is enough stress and anxiety in our world without trying to remember where you placed your car keys eight hours ago when you came into work! Put a carabiner on your purse, bag, or even your belt loop, and you've SOLVED this problem!

Grocery Shopping

Standardize your Lists

Create your list the same way every time so you don't forget anything.

Veggies	Dairy	Meat
Clean	Miscellaneous	

Subscription Services

Hate running out of diapers, dog food, or deodorant ALL the time? Mistake proof it by using the subscription feature from any of the major online retailers. They will automatically ship these items to you as often as you choose, so you never run out.

Home and Family Management

Calendar

Always missing an engagement, doctor's appointment, or kids' event? Mistake proof it by putting everything in your digital calendar. If you have an email address, you have an online calendar that is associated with it. Set the reminder when you create your calendar event, and you will get an email reminder 15, 30, or 60 minutes before the event begins. For events I *really* don't want to miss, I also send an invite to my hubby. That way we both get the reminders of what is happening.

Closet

Is your closet a disaster? You might want to go back and read the 5S section again! I use **visual management by regrouping my pants**. Jeans are on the left. Riding pants are in the middle section and dress pants on the right. For all of the hangers for my riding pants, I have a large neon pink label on the hanger. That way I can quickly see the "dividing line" between the pant types, and easily grab what I need.

Detergent - That Sticky Cap

When we do laundry (you will hear a lot about laundry in this book), we use liquid laundry detergent. You know, the giant, sort of squarish container, that comes with a plastic cup? Every time we use it we first tilt the container forward because we store it on its back with the dispenser up on the top, and we do this so the dispenser doesn't leak laundry detergent all over the floor. Once we fill the cup with detergent, we flip the container on its back, every, single time. We pour the detergent into the designated location in the washer (see...standardize), and then we toss the cup in with the load.

Yes, we **toss the laundry detergent cup in with the load of laundry!** Why? Because it gets super gross, super fast with liquid detergent. Plus, I am super klutzy, and having that cup is an accident waiting to happen with its few drops of detergent and sticky residue. Each load, every time, the cup goes in with the wash and comes out sparkling clean at the end of the cycle.

Laundry Loads

Where are you currently batching and seeing issues emerge? Are you batching your laundry, and finding pink underwear that used to be white? The answer is not to abandon batches and implement one piece flow, or it would take a REALLY long time to wash clothes for a house with four people! Maybe you need to change the way that you batch your laundry loads. Load colors, towels, whites, and delicates, instead of just a batch of colors and whites.

Leftovers

In our refrigerator the second shelf on the right is the designated shelf for leftovers. I even printed a label for that shelf. Each time we have leftovers the containers have their place in the fridge, and now there is no question what is available to eat!

Homework

Make a chart to keep track of your kids' homework assignments. Each one of your kids gets a different color sticky note. Lilly has yellow, Brent has blue, and Sawyer has teal. Each week, every child lists the assignments that are due on individual notecards, and they place them in the *To Do* column.

During the week, as they are physically working on their assignments, they then move the corresponding notecard from the *To Do* column to the *Doing* column. As they finish, complete, or submit their work for that assignment, they then move the card from the *Doing* column to the *Done* column.

You could have a quick family meeting every morning to review the status of the board and to help keep everyone on track. Something inside of us feels so satisfied when we move those notes from one stage to the next, and especially when we move it to the *Done* column. At the end of the week celebrate their accomplishments.

No Dryer, Please!

Do you have washable items that should not, under any circumstances, go into the dryer? These can be hard to keep track of, especially if you may or may not let the laundry sit in the washer for a day or two, or if you are not always the person that moves the laundry from the washer to the dryer.

Use a dry erase marker to write special instructions directly on the dryer.

Get a dry erase marker with a magnet on the back (or glue a magnet to the back of one you already have), and place that marker on top of your washer or dryer. Now when you toss those unmentionables into the wash, or those items that better not go in the dryer or they'll shrink smaller than your pinky toe, use the dry erase marker to write on the top of the dryer "No bras in the dryer" or "No football pads in the dryer."

When anyone moves the load from one machine to the other, they will see this sign and act accordingly. Easy solution. Not every solution has to be complicated or expensive, just remember to erase it before your next load of laundry (standardize and sustain at work, right here!).

Office Issues

Organizing your Emails

I LOVE to use color coding, labels, and email rules, for work. When I worked in Corporate America I had a high level of anxiety about missing an email from my boss. I received hundreds of emails per day, and in that sea of messages, one tiny little email from my boss could easily get missed. I knew, in the sea of black and white, I can easily pick out an email with green color.

I used an email rule in Outlook that allowed me to do two things: 1) Color code the email coming in from my boss to green, and 2) auto-place that email at the top of my email box so it was the first email I saw. Problem solved!

Organizing your Online Calendar

The other thing that caused me anxiety (okay, there were more than two things that caused me anxiety in Corporate America… let's be real here) was missing an important meeting. This can be fixed, too.

I started to color code my meeting invitations. In Outlook you can set the category name for each color in the calendar. For Gmail you just have to remember which color you are using for what reason. On my calendar any meeting sent from my boss would be green. Any events that I was leading were in red. Anything personal (come on, we all block our calendar for personal things) was in pink. I followed (and still follow) this process for every meeting request I accept or create, and it works. This process keeps me organized, and it prevents me from missing important meetings. At a quick glance I can see what my week looks like.

If you can apply improvement concepts at home first, you will find it much easier to apply them at work. How do you organize your emails or your online calendar at work?

Passwords

Like many of us, I have too many passwords to actually remember. I follow the "rules" and every single password I have is different. Gone are the days of using Password123 as your password (kidding, not kidding). You also can't write them on the sticky note under your computer, because there are too many to fit. I use 5S and a little technology to manage my passwords.

- Sort: Try to find all of the pieces of paper where I have written down my passwords and put them in a pile. Determine which ones I use on a consistent basis and which ones I don't (keep and toss pile).
- Set in Order: I review my keep pile, and I do some research on options for storing passwords. (I particularly like a few of the online applications that only require you to remember one password to access the rest of them.) I strongly suggest that you don't save your passwords to your computer, and you don't physically write them down anywhere. (Sorry, the IT person in me is coming out. She can't be quiet when we're talking about this.)
- Shine: Now that you have determined how you are going to store your passwords for easy future reference, start to get organized and review the application so you know what you are doing.
- Standardize: Enter your passwords into your new system. Keep all of the entries the same, including the name of the software, what it's used for, and then your password. Most applications will do this for you.
- Sustain: The hardest part: keep it up! As you acquire new passwords to systems or apps, ensure that you are also updating your new system with your current information.

Visual Management

How can you use visual management at work? Besides creating easily understood signage (like the popular one for "mask required"), you can display some of your metrics on a TV with easy to understand indicators for good (green) or bad (red).

You can implement system notifications so that, as soon as a user logs into a system, they will get an indicator of whether or not action needs to be taken (like completing that required annual training...again). Physical or electronic boards can indicate the status of a team member's work or an order.

Visual management can even be applied to virtual sessions/ video conferencing. Do you want your audience to pay attention to you and your presentation on the screen, or the messy room behind you? Even your presentation slides can be converted to more visual, engaging events, rather than death by bullet points.

Running Reports

Tired of worrying about that compliance report, all the manual work in Excel, and obsessing if you made a mistake? **Mistake proof it through automation and testing!** Then that report will run on its own with zero mistakes.

Travel with Ease

Anytime I travel I use a bright red, letter-sized plastic envelope with a Velcro closure, an item available online or at any office supply store near you. I place all of my travel documents, boarding passes, etc., in the red envelope before I set off on my adventures. This way I can reach into the vast cavern of my backpack to quickly find it, not only because it is red, but also because the slippery, plastic texture is different than anything else in my bag. I can literally reach into my bag and find it without looking.

As I am traveling, I put all of my receipts in that same red folder. At the end of the trip I have everything contained to log in my expenses when I get back home. This prevents me from fumbling around at the ticket gate trying to remember where I placed my boarding pass, and searching through pockets, bags, purses, and suitcases to find all of my receipts.

---

[1] That, my friends, is how you implement the 5S concepts in real life. (More to come on that in a bit.)

[2] True story: I once worked with a client who needed to complete a financial report on a quarterly basis. The process was entirely manual with Excel spreadsheets, system downloads, pivot tables, lookups—every Excel trick in the bag. He needed 19 hours to complete the report, and this often included working through the weekend. The process definitely had some time-consuming issues. We wrote out all of the steps in the process, specifically looking for areas we could quickly improve and automate. We followed PDCA, and in less than a week, he had a completely automated report (including error checking). The absolute BEST part of this story: the manual task that once required 19 hours was consolidated to an automated process that took less than two minutes. Stunning, isn't it?!

[3] Technically, since we start with the letter P, the tool should be called POCIS. Don't ask me why it's called one thing, and then we jumble up the letters to actually complete it. I have spent too many hours of research on this, and I ended up with zero answers to that question.

[4] If you don't have a whiteboard, you can use a Wizard Wall (a whiteboard on a roll), MS Teams whiteboard, Miro.com, or Mural.com (just to name a few). I don't recommend using Visio, as something weird happens in our brain when we have such a structured tool to start. Give your imagination room to breathe.

[5] For more ideas, see the Facebook page for *How to Improve Absolutely Anything.*

[6] Again, if you don't have a whiteboard, you can use the Wizard Wall, a whiteboard on a roll. You can also use a MS Teams whiteboard, Miro.com or Mural.com.

[7] You can find this resource on the How to Improve Absolutely Anything Facebook page.

---

[1] Roderick A Munro, Govindarajan Ramu, Daniel Zrymiak, *The Certified Six Sigma Green Belt Handbook Second Edition* (Milwaukee, WI: ASQ Quality Press, 2015),31

[2] Thomas Pyzdek & Paul Keller, *The Six Sigma Handbook Third Edition* (New York: McGraw Hill, 2010), 3

[3] Paul Akers, 2 Second Lean How to Grow People and Build a Fun Lean Culture (USA: FastCapPress, 2012), 428

[4] James P Womack and Daniel T Jones, *Lean Thinking* (New York: Free Press, 1996),61

[5] Psycho-Cybernetics, Dr. Maxwell Maltz

[6] How Long Does it Take to Form a Habit? 21 Days? 66 Days? (developgoodhabits.com)

[7] What Is A Minimum Viable Product, And Why Do Companies Need Them? (forbes.com)

[8] Govind Ramu, *The Certified Six Sigma Yellow Belt Handbook* (Milwaukee, WI: ASQ Quality Press,2017),122

[9] Robert O. Martichenko, *Everything I Know About Lean I Learned In First Grade* (Cambridge, MA: Lean Enterprise Institute, 2008),80

[10] John Morgan and Martin Brenig-Jones, *Lean Six Sigma for Dummies Second Edition* (Chichester, England: John Wiley & Sons, Ltd, 2012), 1166

[11] Lawrence G Fine, *The SWOT Analysis Using Strengths to overcome Weaknesses Using Opportunities to overcome Threats* (Kick It, LLC, 2011), 9

[12] Toni Krasnic, *How to Study with Mind Maps Concise Learning Method* (Concise Books Publishing, 2012), 52

[13] Law of Diminishing Marginal Returns (Investopedia.com)

[14] (Ebbinghaus Curve or the Forgetting Curve, Hermann Ebbinghaus).

[15] Michael George, David Rowlands, Mark Price, John Maxey, *The Lean Six Sigma Pocket Toolbook* (New York: McGraw Hill, 2005), 146

[16] Thomas Pyzdek and Paul Keller, *Six Sigma Handbook Fourth Edition* (Chennai: McGraw Hill, 2014), 427

[17] Thomas Pyzdek and Paul Keller, *Six Sigma Handbook Fourth Edition* (Chennai: McGraw Hill, 2014), 431

[18] Roderick A Munro, Govindarajan Ramu, Daniel Zrymiak, *The Certified Six Sigma Green Belt Handbook Second Edition* (Milwaukee, WI: ASQ Quality Press, 2015), 353

[19] Thomas Pyzdek & Paul Keller, *The Six Sigma Handbook Third Edition* (New York: McGraw Hill, 2010), 3

[20] Hourly History, *Henry Ford: A Life From Beginning to End (Biographies of Business Leaders Book 3)* (Hourly History, 2017), 3

[21] Using the Stages of Team Development (hr.mit.edu)

ABOUT THE AUTHOR

Katie Labedz

Hi! I'm Katie Labedz. I am a mid-west girl who loves sunshine, horses, and riding across the country with my husband on our motorcycles. I have a passion for helping people improve their everyday tasks, both at work and at home. I believe that if you can understand how to improve your personal life with continuous improvement concepts, then you can apply those concepts in every sphere of your life. That's why I wrote this book: to make the concepts of continuous improvement work for you.

Now for the professional part: I am a Lean Six Sigma Master Black Belt, certified project management professional, certified instructor/facilitator, professional speaker, author, instructional designer, coach, and mentor—and I have a degree in Management Information Systems. I worked in Corporate America for most of my career, and I am now the president of my own continuous improvement consulting firm, Learning to Lean LLC.

Printed in Dunstable, United Kingdom

84489861R00080